# DIBELS® Next Progress Monitoring Assessment Book B: Assessor Directions and Student Materials

Roland H. Good III

Ruth A. Kaminski

*with:* Kelli Cummings, Chantal Dufour-Martel, Kathleen Petersen,
Kelly Powell-Smith, Stephanie Stollar, and Joshua Wallin

Dynamic Measurement Group, Inc.

DIBELS is a registered trademark of Dynamic Measurement Group, Inc. Visit our Web site at www.dibels.org.

(Revised: 04/06/10)

| PSF | NWF | DORF/Level 1 | DORF/Level 2 | DORF/Le... |

ISBN 13: 978-1-60697-389-9
ISBN 10: 1-60697-389-4

27321O/354/03-12

Printed in the United States of America

Published and Distributed by

4093 Specialty Place • Longmont, Colorado 80504
(303) 651-2829 • www.soprislearning.com

# How to Use This Book

This book includes the necessary student materials and the directions for administering each measure to students. Before administering the progress monitoring assessment, be sure you have read the *DIBELS Next Assessment Manual* and have practiced administering these measures so that you are comfortable using them with students.

You will also need one copy of the appropriate Progress Monitoring Scoring Booklet for each student, to record the student's responses and scores.

Phoneme Segmentation Fluency does not include student materials. For this measure, read the instructions from this book and read the test items from the scoring booklet.

During testing, this book should lay flat on a desk or table, with the student materials placed directly in front of the student. The assessor directions and instructions to read to the student are located on the opposite page for ease of use. Be sure to remove any other possible distractions from the testing surface.

Please refer to the *DIBELS Next Assessment Manual* for more information on administering and scoring each *DIBELS Next* measure.

| PSF | NWF | DORF/Level 1 | DORF/Level 2 | DORF/Level 3 |

# Table of Contents

**Directions:** Make sure you have reviewed the scoring rules in the *DIBELS Next Assessment Manual* and have them available. Say these specific directions to the student:

▶ **We are going to say the sounds in words. Listen to me say all the sounds in the word "fan."** */f/ /a/ /n/.* **Listen to another word,** (pause) **"jump."** */j/ /u/ /m/ /p/.* **Your turn. Say all the sounds in "soap."**

| | | |
|---|---|---|
| *Correct response* /s/ /oa/ /p/ | **Very good saying all the sounds in "soap."** | (Begin testing.) |

| | | | | |
|---|---|---|---|---|
| *Incorrect response* anything other than /s/ /oa/ /p/ | **I said "soap," so you say /s/ /oa/ /p/. Your turn. Say all the sounds in "soap."** | *Correct response* | **Very good.** | (Begin testing.) |
| | | *Incorrect response* | **Okay.** | (Begin testing.) |

▶ **Begin testing. *I am going to say more words. I will say the word, and you say all the sounds in the word.*** (Say the first word from the list in the scoring booklet.)

| | |
|---|---|
| **Timing** | 1 minute. Start your stopwatch after saying the first test item. |
| **Wait** | If the student does not respond within 3 seconds, say the next word. |
| **Discontinue** | If no sound segments are correct in the first five words, discontinue and record a score of 0. |
| **Reminders** | If the student spells the word, say **Say the <u>sounds</u> in the word.** Immediately say the next word. (Allowed one time.) |
| | If the student repeats the word, say **Remember to say all the sounds in the word.** Immediately say the next word. (Allowed one time.) |

sog          mip

# 1 DIBELS® Nonsense Word Fluency
Progress Monitoring 1

**Directions:** Make sure you have reviewed the scoring rules in the *DIBELS Next Assessment Manual* and have them available. Say these specific directions to the student:

▶ *We are going to read some make-believe words. Listen. This word is "sog."* (Run your finger under the word as you say it.) *The sounds are /s/ /o/ /g/* (point to each letter). *Your turn. Read this make-believe word* (point to the word "mip"). *If you can't read the whole word, tell me any sounds you know.*

| Correct Whole Word Read<br>mip | **Very good reading the word "mip."** | (Begin testing.) | |
|---|---|---|---|
| Correct Letter Sounds<br>Any other response with all the correct letter sounds | **Very good. /m/ /i/ /p/** (point to each letter) **or "mip"** (run your finger under the word as you say it)**.** | (Begin testing.) | |

| Incorrect response<br>No response within 3 <u>seconds</u>, or response includes any errors | **Listen. /m/ /i/ /p/ or "mip."** (Run your finger under the letters as you say the sounds.) **Your turn. Read this make-believe word.** (Point to the word "mip.") **If you can't read the whole word, tell me any sounds you know.** | Correct response | **Very good.** (Begin testing.) |
| | | Incorrect response | **Okay.** (Begin testing.) |

▶ **Begin testing.** *I would like you to read more make-believe words. Do your best reading. If you can't read the whole word, tell me any sounds you know.* Go to the next page.

| | | | | |
|---|---|---|---|---|
| ▶ hif | mez | un | jaf | roc |
| liv | rem | vam | ov | luf |
| yej | lig | zat | hof | puj |
| ib | maj | wos | keb | ruk |
| ug | jin | pag | bom | sez |
| des | woj | lut | rav | zil |
| kun | aj | yim | rev | kol |
| huf | soz | zas | dif | em |
| ked | tov | zuv | paf | jip |
| vap | id | muj | sec | sol |

# 1 DIBELS® Nonsense Word Fluency
Progress Monitoring 1 continued

▶ *Put your finger under the first word. Ready, begin.*

| | |
|---|---|
| **Timing** | 1 minute. Start your stopwatch after telling the student to begin. Place a bracket ( **]** ) and say *Stop* after 1 minute. |
| **Wait** | If the student responds sound-by-sound, mixes sounds and words, or sounds out and recodes, allow 3 seconds, then provide the correct letter sound. |
| | If the student responds with whole words, allow 3 seconds, then provide the correct word. |
| **Discontinue** | If the student has no correct letter sounds in the first line, say *Stop* and record a score of 0. |
| **Reminders** | If the student does not read from left to right, say *Go this way*. (Sweep your finger across the row.) (Allowed one time.) |
| | If the student says letter names, say *Say the sounds, not the letter names*. (Allowed one time.) |
| | If the student reads the word first, then says the letter sounds, say *Just read the word*. (Allowed one time.) |
| | If the student says all of the letter sounds correctly in the first row, but does not make any attempt to blend or recode, say *Try to read the words as whole words*. |
| | If the student stops (and it's not a hesitation on a specific item), say *Keep going*. (Repeat as often as needed.) |
| | If the student loses his/her place, point. (Repeat as often as needed.) |

NWF

sog        mip

# 2 DIBELS® Nonsense Word Fluency
## Progress Monitoring 2

*Directions:* Make sure you have reviewed the scoring rules in the *DIBELS Next Assessment Manual* and have them available. Say these specific directions to the student:

---

► *We are going to read some make-believe words. Listen. This word is "sog."* (Run your finger under the word as you say it.) *The sounds are /s/ /o/ /g/* (point to each letter). *Your turn. Read this make-believe word* (point to the word "mip"). *If you can't read the whole word, tell me any sounds you know.*

| Correct Whole Word Read mip | **Very good reading the word "mip."** | (Begin testing.) | | |
|---|---|---|---|---|
| Correct Letter Sounds Any other response with all the correct letter sounds | **Very good. /m/ /i/ /p/** (point to each letter) **or "mip"** (run your finger under the word as you say it). | (Begin testing.) | | |
| Incorrect response No response within 3 <u>seconds</u>, or response includes any errors | **Listen. /m/ /i/ /p/ or "mip."** (Run your finger under the letters as you say the sounds.) **Your turn. Read this make-believe word.** (Point to the word "mip.") **If you can't read the whole word, tell me any sounds you know.** | Correct response | **Very good.** | (Begin testing.) |
| | | Incorrect response | **Okay.** | (Begin testing.) |

► Begin testing. *I would like you to read more make-believe words. Do your best reading. If you can't read the whole word, tell me any sounds you know.* Go to the next page.

| | | | | |
|---|---|---|---|---|
| ▶ ris | baj | uk | zom | het |
| foj | muc | yeb | iv | baf |
| yaz | mol | zet | pid | luv |
| im | loz | jeg | kal | fub |
| ot | juf | fal | neb | diz |
| huc | wiv | mes | pav | zol |
| dus | oj | jes | tiz | mak |
| rud | sej | wac | mis | os |
| bis | bez | jav | tuf | joc |
| zin | ub | tej | bal | lof |

# 2 DIBELS® Nonsense Word Fluency
Progress Monitoring 2 continued

▶ *Put your finger under the first word. Ready, begin.*

| | |
|---|---|
| **Timing** | 1 minute. Start your stopwatch after telling the student to begin. Place a bracket ( ] ) and say **Stop** after 1 minute. |
| **Wait** | If the student responds sound-by-sound, mixes sounds and words, or sounds out and recodes, allow 3 seconds, then provide the correct letter sound.<br><br>If the student responds with whole words, allow 3 seconds, then provide the correct word. |
| **Discontinue** | If the student has no correct letter sounds in the first line, say **Stop** and record a score of 0. |
| **Reminders** | If the student does not read from left to right, say **Go this way**. (Sweep your finger across the row.) (Allowed one time.)<br><br>If the student says letter names, say **Say the sounds, not the letter names**. (Allowed one time.)<br><br>If the student reads the word first, then says the letter sounds, say **Just read the word**. (Allowed one time.)<br><br>If the student says all of the letter sounds correctly in the first row, but does not make any attempt to blend or recode, say **Try to read the words as whole words**.<br><br>If the student stops (and it's not a hesitation on a specific item), say **Keep going**. (Repeat as often as needed.)<br><br>If the student loses his/her place, point. (Repeat as often as needed.) |

sog          mip

# 3 DIBELS® Nonsense Word Fluency
Progress Monitoring 3

**Directions:** Make sure you have reviewed the scoring rules in the *DIBELS Next Assessment Manual* and have them available. Say these specific directions to the student:

---

▶ *We are going to read some make-believe words. Listen. This word is "sog."* (Run your finger under the word as you say it.) *The sounds are /s/ /o/ /g/* (point to each letter). *Your turn. Read this make-believe word* (point to the word "mip"). *If you can't read the whole word, tell me any sounds you know.*

| | | |
|---|---|---|
| *Correct Whole Word Read* mip | ***Very good reading the word "mip."*** | (Begin testing.) |
| *Correct Letter Sounds* Any other response with all the correct letter sounds | ***Very good. /m/ /i/ /p/*** (point to each letter) ***or "mip"*** (run your finger under the word as you say it). | (Begin testing.) |

| | | | | |
|---|---|---|---|---|
| *Incorrect response* No response within 3 <u>seconds</u>, or response includes any errors | ***Listen. /m/ /i/ /p/ or "mip."*** (Run your finger under the letters as you say the sounds.) ***Your turn. Read this make-believe word.*** (Point to the word "mip.") ***If you can't read the whole word, tell me any sounds you know.*** | *Correct response* | **Very good.** | (Begin testing.) |
| | | *Incorrect response* | **Okay.** | (Begin testing.) |

▶ **Begin testing.** *I would like you to read more make-believe words. Do your best reading. If you can't read the whole word, tell me any sounds you know.* **Go to the next page.**

▶ sek     tav     og     yuk     lil

mav     nef     vif     uz     non

jez     fid     yud     mot     sav

ep     poz     zal     suf     bil

od     vil     teb     nuc     nav

dep     zoj     ras     luz     wic

bof     ev     zun     fav     mim

dom     tiv     zes     haf     un

lol     nij     jaj     puc     zem

yef     um     miv     pof     pac

## 3 DIBELS® Nonsense Word Fluency
Progress Monitoring 3 continued

▶ *Put your finger under the first word. Ready, begin.*

| | |
|---|---|
| *Timing* | 1 minute. Start your stopwatch after telling the student to begin. Place a bracket ( **]** ) and say **Stop** after 1 minute. |
| *Wait* | If the student responds sound-by-sound, mixes sounds and words, or sounds out and recodes, allow 3 seconds, then provide the correct letter sound.<br><br>If the student responds with whole words, allow 3 seconds, then provide the correct word. |
| *Discontinue* | If the student has no correct letter sounds in the first line, say **Stop** and record a score of 0. |
| *Reminders* | If the student does not read from left to right, say **Go this way**. (Sweep your finger across the row.) (Allowed one time.)<br><br>If the student says letter names, say **Say the sounds, not the letter names**. (Allowed one time.)<br><br>If the student reads the word first, then says the letter sounds, say **Just read the word**. (Allowed one time.)<br><br>If the student says all of the letter sounds correctly in the first row, but does not make any attempt to blend or recode, say **Try to read the words as whole words**.<br><br>If the student stops (and it's not a hesitation on a specific item), say **Keep going**. (Repeat as often as needed.)<br><br>If the student loses his/her place, point. (Repeat as often as needed.) |

NWF

sog          mip

# 4 DIBELS® Nonsense Word Fluency
Progress Monitoring 4

**Directions:** Make sure you have reviewed the scoring rules in the *DIBELS Next Assessment Manual* and have them available. Say these specific directions to the student:

---

▶ *We are going to read some make-believe words. Listen. This word is "sog."* (Run your finger under the word as you say it.) *The sounds are /s/ /o/ /g/* (point to each letter). *Your turn. Read this make-believe word* (point to the word "mip"). *If you can't read the whole word, tell me any sounds you know.*

| | | |
|---|---|---|
| Correct Whole Word Read<br>mip | ***Very good reading the word "mip."*** | (Begin testing.) |

| | | |
|---|---|---|
| Correct Letter Sounds<br>Any other response with all the correct letter sounds | ***Very good. /m/ /i/ /p/*** (point to each letter) ***or "mip"*** (run your finger under the word as you say it). | (Begin testing.) |

| | | | | |
|---|---|---|---|---|
| Incorrect response<br>No response within 3 <u>seconds</u>, or response includes any errors | ***Listen. /m/ /i/ /p/ or "mip."*** (Run your finger under the letters as you say the sounds.) ***Your turn. Read this make-believe word.*** (Point to the word "mip.") ***If you can't read the whole word, tell me any sounds you know.*** | Correct response | **Very good.** | (Begin testing.) |
| | | Incorrect response | **Okay.** | (Begin testing.) |

▶ Begin testing. *I would like you to read more make-believe words. Do your best reading. If you can't read the whole word, tell me any sounds you know.* Go to the next page.

NWF

| | | | | |
|---|---|---|---|---|
| ▶ lun | naj | ec | zob | tig |
| bov | fim | vac | uj | hed |
| wov | dek | vun | hac | riv |
| af | huz | vim | seg | nop |
| oc | zeb | kam | tul | hiz |
| nad | zez | rop | ruj | wis |
| lak | ij | wun | boz | kec |
| pib | bav | wuc | bol | ek |
| meb | maj | juv | dit | zok |
| yec | ob | niz | buc | rak |

# 4 DIBELS® Nonsense Word Fluency
Progress Monitoring 4 continued

▶ *Put your finger under the first word. Ready, begin.*

| | |
|---|---|
| **Timing** | 1 minute. Start your stopwatch after telling the student to begin. Place a bracket ( **]** ) and say **Stop** after 1 minute. |
| **Wait** | If the student responds sound-by-sound, mixes sounds and words, or sounds out and recodes, allow 3 seconds, then provide the correct letter sound. |
| | If the student responds with whole words, allow 3 seconds, then provide the correct word. |
| **Discontinue** | If the student has no correct letter sounds in the first line, say **Stop** and record a score of 0. |
| **Reminders** | If the student does not read from left to right, say **Go this way**. (Sweep your finger across the row.) (Allowed one time.) |
| | If the student says letter names, say **Say the sounds, not the letter names**. (Allowed one time.) |
| | If the student reads the word first, then says the letter sounds, say **Just read the word**. (Allowed one time.) |
| | If the student says all of the letter sounds correctly in the first row, but does not make any attempt to blend or recode, say **Try to read the words as whole words**. |
| | If the student stops (and it's not a hesitation on a specific item), say **Keep going**. (Repeat as often as needed.) |
| | If the student loses his/her place, point. (Repeat as often as needed.) |

sog     mip

# 5 DIBELS® Nonsense Word Fluency
Progress Monitoring 5

**Directions:** Make sure you have reviewed the scoring rules in the *DIBELS Next Assessment Manual* and have them available. Say these specific directions to the student:

▶ *We are going to read some make-believe words. Listen. This word is "sog."* (Run your finger under the word as you say it.) *The sounds are /s/ /o/ /g/* (point to each letter). *Your turn. Read this make-believe word* (point to the word "mip"). *If you can't read the whole word, tell me any sounds you know.*

| | | |
|---|---|---|
| *Correct Whole Word Read* <br> mip | **Very good reading the word "mip."** | (Begin testing.) |
| *Correct Letter Sounds* <br> Any other response with all the correct letter sounds | **Very good. /m/ /i/ /p/** (point to each letter) **or "mip"** (run your finger under the word as you say it). | (Begin testing.) |

| | | | | |
|---|---|---|---|---|
| *Incorrect response* <br> No response within 3 <u>seconds</u>, or response includes any errors | **Listen. /m/ /i/ /p/ or "mip."** (Run your finger under the letters as you say the sounds.) **Your turn. Read this make-believe word.** (Point to the word "mip.") **If you can't read the whole word, tell me any sounds you know.** | *Correct response* | **Very good.** | (Begin testing.) |
| | | *Incorrect response* | **Okay.** | (Begin testing.) |

▶ **Begin testing.** *I would like you to read more make-believe words. Do your best reading. If you can't read the whole word, tell me any sounds you know.* Go to the next page.

| | | | | |
|---|---|---|---|---|
| ▶ lim | saj | ug | yot | fep |
| dej | tas | yop | ij | dun |
| zov | sal | yit | ped | muv |
| ic | kav | veg | dop | kuk |
| ul | waf | pok | mel | biv |
| ret | vuv | hin | roj | jad |
| fen | av | zot | biz | lud |
| sug | dij | yat | nog | el |
| mef | piz | zav | pul | zof |
| wob | em | hij | kas | kuc |

▶ *Put your finger under the first word. Ready, begin.*

| | |
|---|---|
| **Timing** | 1 minute. Start your stopwatch after telling the student to begin. Place a bracket ( ] ) and say **Stop** after 1 minute. |
| **Wait** | If the student responds sound-by-sound, mixes sounds and words, or sounds out and recodes, allow 3 seconds, then provide the correct letter sound. |
| | If the student responds with whole words, allow 3 seconds, then provide the correct word. |
| **Discontinue** | If the student has no correct letter sounds in the first line, say **Stop** and record a score of 0. |
| **Reminders** | If the student does not read from left to right, say **Go this way**. (Sweep your finger across the row.) (Allowed one time.) |
| | If the student says letter names, say **Say the sounds, not the letter names**. (Allowed one time.) |
| | If the student reads the word first, then says the letter sounds, say **Just read the word**. (Allowed one time.) |
| | If the student says all of the letter sounds correctly in the first row, but does not make any attempt to blend or recode, say **Try to read the words as whole words**. |
| | If the student stops (and it's not a hesitation on a specific item), say **Keep going**. (Repeat as often as needed.) |
| | If the student loses his/her place, point. (Repeat as often as needed.) |

NWF

sog         mip

# 6 DIBELS® Nonsense Word Fluency
Progress Monitoring 6

***Directions:*** Make sure you have reviewed the scoring rules in the *DIBELS Next Assessment Manual* and have them available. Say these specific directions to the student:

► ***We are going to read some make-believe words. Listen. This word is "sog."*** (Run your finger under the word as you say it.) ***The sounds are /s/ /o/ /g/*** (point to each letter). ***Your turn. Read this make-believe word*** (point to the word "mip"). ***If you can't read the whole word, tell me any sounds you know.***

| | | | | |
|---|---|---|---|---|
| *Correct Whole Word Read*<br>mip | ***Very good reading the word "mip."*** | | (Begin testing.) | |
| *Correct Letter Sounds*<br>Any other response with all the correct letter sounds | ***Very good. /m/ /i/ /p/*** (point to each letter) ***or "mip"*** (run your finger under the word as you say it). | | (Begin testing.) | |
| *Incorrect response*<br>No response within 3 <u>seconds</u>, or response includes any errors | ***Listen. /m/ /i/ /p/ or "mip."*** (Run your finger under the letters as you say the sounds.) ***Your turn. Read this make-believe word.*** (Point to the word "mip.") ***If you can't read the whole word, tell me any sounds you know.*** | *Correct response* | ***Very good.*** | (Begin testing.) |
| | | *Incorrect response* | ***Okay.*** | (Begin testing.) |

► **Begin testing.** *I would like you to read more make-believe words. Do your best reading. If you can't read the whole word, tell me any sounds you know.* **Go to the next page.**

*DIBELS® Next Progress Monitoring Assessment Book B*

**NWF**

23

| hos | bev | ab | zut | mig |
|-----|-----|-----|-----|-----|
| pav | loc | yeg | uj | tid |
| jev | sif | jop | tac | tuz |
| ib | mev | jus | bac | kon |
| ud | vaf | kel | fod | riz |
| ses | yuj | mon | rij | vad |
| dat | iv | zuf | lov | neg |
| bas | miz | jom | mep | uc |
| rik | fez | zuj | pon | wam |
| zon | id | fej | maf | duk |

▶ *Put your finger under the first word. Ready, begin.*

| | |
|---|---|
| *Timing* | 1 minute. Start your stopwatch after telling the student to begin. Place a bracket ( **]** ) and say **Stop** after 1 minute. |
| *Wait* | If the student responds sound-by-sound, mixes sounds and words, or sounds out and recodes, allow 3 seconds, then provide the correct letter sound. |
| | If the student responds with whole words, allow 3 seconds, then provide the correct word. |
| *Discontinue* | If the student has no correct letter sounds in the first line, say **Stop** and record a score of 0. |
| *Reminders* | If the student does not read from left to right, say **Go this way**. (Sweep your finger across the row.) (Allowed one time.) |
| | If the student says letter names, say **Say the sounds, not the letter names**. (Allowed one time.) |
| | If the student reads the word first, then says the letter sounds, say **Just read the word**. (Allowed one time.) |
| | If the student says all of the letter sounds correctly in the first row, but does not make any attempt to blend or recode, say **Try to read the words as whole words**. |
| | If the student stops (and it's not a hesitation on a specific item), say **Keep going**. (Repeat as often as needed.) |
| | If the student loses his/her place, point. (Repeat as often as needed.) |

sog                    mip

# 7 DIBELS® Nonsense Word Fluency
Progress Monitoring 7

***Directions:*** Make sure you have reviewed the scoring rules in the *DIBELS Next Assessment Manual* and have them available. Say these specific directions to the student:

▶ *We are going to read some make-believe words. Listen. This word is "sog."* (Run your finger under the word as you say it.) *The sounds are /s/ /o/ /g/* (point to each letter). *Your turn. Read this make-believe word* (point to the word "mip"). *If you can't read the whole word, tell me any sounds you know.*

| | | |
|---|---|---|
| *Correct Whole Word Read* mip | ***Very good reading the word "mip."*** | (Begin testing.) |

| | | | | |
|---|---|---|---|---|
| *Correct Letter Sounds* Any other response with all the correct letter sounds | ***Very good. /m/ /i/ /p/*** (point to each letter) ***or "mip"*** (run your finger under the word as you say it)***.*** | (Begin testing.) | | |

| | | | | |
|---|---|---|---|---|
| *Incorrect response* No response within 3 <u>seconds</u>, or response includes any errors | ***Listen. /m/ /i/ /p/ or "mip."*** (Run your finger under the letters as you say the sounds.) ***Your turn. Read this make-believe word.*** (Point to the word "mip.") ***If you can't read the whole word, tell me any sounds you know.*** | *Correct response* | ***Very good.*** | (Begin testing.) |
| | | *Incorrect response* | ***Okay.*** | (Begin testing.) |

▶ **Begin testing.** *I would like you to read more make-believe words. Do your best reading. If you can't read the whole word, tell me any sounds you know.* **Go to the next page.**

| | | | | |
|---|---|---|---|---|
| ▶ nim | duz | ak | zek | dok |
| rav | lin | vod | ev | nus |
| vez | kac | yib | duc | hoj |
| op | tij | jak | det | nup |
| ef | yof | pik | nub | laj |
| sok | yij | def | raj | vus |
| faf | oj | weg | niv | lum |
| fom | kij | wal | mec | ut |
| lef | mij | vuj | mog | vas |
| vib | ap | ruz | reg | mof |

# 7 DIBELS® Nonsense Word Fluency
Progress Monitoring 7 continued

▶ *Put your finger under the first word. Ready, begin.*

| | |
|---|---|
| *Timing* | 1 minute. Start your stopwatch after telling the student to begin. Place a bracket ( **]** ) and say *Stop* after 1 minute. |
| *Wait* | If the student responds sound-by-sound, mixes sounds and words, or sounds out and recodes, allow 3 seconds, then provide the correct letter sound.<br><br>If the student responds with whole words, allow 3 seconds, then provide the correct word. |
| *Discontinue* | If the student has no correct letter sounds in the first line, say *Stop* and record a score of 0. |
| *Reminders* | If the student does not read from left to right, say *Go this way*. (Sweep your finger across the row.) (Allowed one time.)<br><br>If the student says letter names, say *Say the sounds, not the letter names*. (Allowed one time.)<br><br>If the student reads the word first, then says the letter sounds, say *Just read the word*. (Allowed one time.)<br><br>If the student says all of the letter sounds correctly in the first row, but does not make any attempt to blend or recode, say *Try to read the words as whole words*.<br><br>If the student stops (and it's not a hesitation on a specific item), say *Keep going*. (Repeat as often as needed.)<br><br>If the student loses his/her place, point. (Repeat as often as needed.) |

sog          mip

# 8 DIBELS® Nonsense Word Fluency
## Progress Monitoring 8

**Directions:** Make sure you have reviewed the scoring rules in the *DIBELS Next Assessment Manual* and have them available. Say these specific directions to the student:

▶ *We are going to read some make-believe words. Listen. This word is "sog."* (Run your finger under the word as you say it.) *The sounds are /s/ /o/ /g/* (point to each letter). *Your turn. Read this make-believe word* (point to the word "mip"). *If you can't read the whole word, tell me any sounds you know.*

| | | |
|---|---|---|
| Correct Whole Word Read<br>mip | *Very good reading the word "mip."* | (Begin testing.) |
| Correct Letter Sounds<br>Any other response with all the correct letter sounds | *Very good. /m/ /i/ /p/* (point to each letter) *or "mip"* (run your finger under the word as you say it). | (Begin testing.) |

| | | | | |
|---|---|---|---|---|
| Incorrect response<br>No response within 3 <u>seconds</u>, or response includes any errors | *Listen. /m/ /i/ /p/ or "mip."* (Run your finger under the letters as you say the sounds.) *Your turn. Read this make-believe word.* (Point to the word "mip.") *If you can't read the whole word, tell me any sounds you know.* | Correct response | *Very good.* | (Begin testing.) |
| | | Incorrect response | *Okay.* | (Begin testing.) |

▶ **Begin testing.** *I would like you to read more make-believe words. Do your best reading. If you can't read the whole word, tell me any sounds you know.* Go to the next page.

| | | | | |
|---|---|---|---|---|
| ▶ nam | muz | et | wom | fip |
| doj | las | zef | uv | fis |
| zoz | tem | vid | lub | faj |
| ag | doz | vis | tuc | pec |
| uf | wik | tet | mod | dav |
| dec | viv | rom | daj | yuf |
| fob | az | zib | fev | ruf |
| hes | koj | wus | kig | ac |
| hal | luj | ziv | kod | wem |
| vut | eb | paj | hib | noc |

▶ *Put your finger under the first word. Ready, begin.*

| | |
|---|---|
| **Timing** | 1 minute. Start your stopwatch after telling the student to begin. Place a bracket ( ] ) and say **Stop** after 1 minute. |
| **Wait** | If the student responds sound-by-sound, mixes sounds and words, or sounds out and recodes, allow 3 seconds, then provide the correct letter sound. |
| | If the student responds with whole words, allow 3 seconds, then provide the correct word. |
| **Discontinue** | If the student has no correct letter sounds in the first line, say **Stop** and record a score of 0. |
| **Reminders** | If the student does not read from left to right, say **Go this way**. (Sweep your finger across the row.) (Allowed one time.) |
| | If the student says letter names, say **Say the sounds, not the letter names**. (Allowed one time.) |
| | If the student reads the word first, then says the letter sounds, say **Just read the word**. (Allowed one time.) |
| | If the student says all of the letter sounds correctly in the first row, but does not make any attempt to blend or recode, say **Try to read the words as whole words**. |
| | If the student stops (and it's not a hesitation on a specific item), say **Keep going**. (Repeat as often as needed.) |
| | If the student loses his/her place, point. (Repeat as often as needed.) |

NWF

sog                    mip

# 9 DIBELS® Nonsense Word Fluency
Progress Monitoring 9

*Directions:* Make sure you have reviewed the scoring rules in the *DIBELS Next Assessment Manual* and have them available. Say these specific directions to the student:

▶ *We are going to read some make-believe words. Listen. This word is "sog."* (Run your finger under the word as you say it.) *The sounds are /s/ /o/ /g/* (point to each letter). *Your turn. Read this make-believe word* (point to the word "mip"). *If you can't read the whole word, tell me any sounds you know.*

| | | |
|---|---|---|
| *Correct Whole Word Read*<br>mip | **Very good reading the word "mip."** | (Begin testing.) |
| *Correct Letter Sounds*<br>Any other response with all the correct letter sounds | **Very good. /m/ /i/ /p/** (point to each letter) **or "mip"** (run your finger under the word as you say it). | (Begin testing.) |

| | | | | |
|---|---|---|---|---|
| *Incorrect response*<br>No response within 3 <u>seconds</u>, or response includes any errors | **Listen. /m/ /i/ /p/ or "mip."** (Run your finger under the letters as you say the sounds.) **Your turn. Read this make-believe word.** (Point to the word "mip.") **If you can't read the whole word, tell me any sounds you know.** | *Correct response* | **Very good.** | (Begin testing.) |
| | | *Incorrect response* | **Okay.** | (Begin testing.) |

▶ **Begin testing.** *I would like you to read more make-believe words. Do your best reading. If you can't read the whole word, tell me any sounds you know.* **Go to the next page.**

| | | | | |
|---|---|---|---|---|
| ▶ sid | buj | eg | vok | hab |
| soj | feg | zac | uz | mid |
| juz | hak | wif | nem | moz |
| ig | koz | jum | nep | kat |
| om | zel | sac | fik | nuz |
| laf | wej | kip | puv | von |
| sas | ov | yic | sev | tum |
| bes | kaj | yug | hil | ol |
| sup | mov | yav | sep | vig |
| jol | en | puz | lac | mil |

# 9 DIBELS® Nonsense Word Fluency
Progress Monitoring 9 continued

▶ *Put your finger under the first word. Ready, begin.*

| | |
|---|---|
| **Timing** | 1 minute. Start your stopwatch after telling the student to begin. Place a bracket ( ] ) and say **Stop** after 1 minute. |
| **Wait** | If the student responds sound-by-sound, mixes sounds and words, or sounds out and recodes, allow 3 seconds, then provide the correct letter sound. |
| | If the student responds with whole words, allow 3 seconds, then provide the correct word. |
| **Discontinue** | If the student has no correct letter sounds in the first line, say **Stop** and record a score of 0. |
| **Reminders** | If the student does not read from left to right, say **Go this way**. (Sweep your finger across the row.) (Allowed one time.) |
| | If the student says letter names, say **Say the sounds, not the letter names**. (Allowed one time.) |
| | If the student reads the word first, then says the letter sounds, say **Just read the word**. (Allowed one time.) |
| | If the student says all of the letter sounds correctly in the first row, but does not make any attempt to blend or recode, say **Try to read the words as whole words**. |
| | If the student stops (and it's not a hesitation on a specific item), say **Keep going**. (Repeat as often as needed.) |
| | If the student loses his/her place, point. (Repeat as often as needed.) |

sog          mip

# 10 DIBELS® Nonsense Word Fluency
Progress Monitoring 10

***Directions:*** Make sure you have reviewed the scoring rules in the *DIBELS Next Assessment Manual* and have them available. Say these specific directions to the student:

---

▶ ***We are going to read some make-believe words. Listen. This word is "sog."*** (Run your finger under the word as you say it.) ***The sounds are /s/ /o/ /g/*** (point to each letter). ***Your turn. Read this make-believe word*** (point to the word "mip"). ***If you can't read the whole word, tell me any sounds you know.***

| | | |
|---|---|---|
| *Correct Whole Word Read* mip | ***Very good reading the word "mip."*** | (Begin testing.) |

| | | |
|---|---|---|
| *Correct Letter Sounds* Any other response with all the correct letter sounds | ***Very good. /m/ /i/ /p/*** (point to each letter) ***or "mip"*** (run your finger under the word as you say it)***.*** | (Begin testing.) |

| | | | | |
|---|---|---|---|---|
| *Incorrect response* No response within 3 <u>seconds</u>, or response includes any errors | ***Listen. /m/ /i/ /p/ or "mip."*** (Run your finger under the letters as you say the sounds.) ***Your turn. Read this make-believe word.*** (Point to the word "mip.") ***If you can't read the whole word, tell me any sounds you know.*** | *Correct response* | ***Very good.*** | (Begin testing.) |
| | | *Incorrect response* | ***Okay.*** | (Begin testing.) |

▶ **Begin testing.** *I would like you to read more make-believe words. Do your best reading. If you can't read the whole word, tell me any sounds you know.* Go to the next page.

| | | | | |
|---|---|---|---|---|
| ▶ sen | nuv | ip | wat | nok |
| nav | pum | ved | iv | fof |
| ziz | tol | zan | duf | nev |
| ut | moj | jeb | tis | mas |
| al | jun | nek | fol | piv |
| hom | jij | kaf | dez | yup |
| sof | ij | jul | taj | hef |
| kem | hoz | zim | sak | un |
| lus | rej | yoj | ral | zis |
| yab | op | pij | sel | tun |

# 10 DIBELS® Nonsense Word Fluency
Progress Monitoring 10 continued

▶ *Put your finger under the first word. Ready, begin.*

| | |
|---|---|
| *Timing* | 1 minute. Start your stopwatch after telling the student to begin. Place a bracket ( **]** ) and say **Stop** after 1 minute. |
| *Wait* | If the student responds sound-by-sound, mixes sounds and words, or sounds out and recodes, allow 3 seconds, then provide the correct letter sound.<br><br>If the student responds with whole words, allow 3 seconds, then provide the correct word. |
| *Discontinue* | If the student has no correct letter sounds in the first line, say **Stop** and record a score of 0. |
| *Reminders* | If the student does not read from left to right, say **Go this way**. (Sweep your finger across the row.) (Allowed one time.)<br><br>If the student says letter names, say **Say the sounds, not the letter names**. (Allowed one time.)<br><br>If the student reads the word first, then says the letter sounds, say **Just read the word**. (Allowed one time.)<br><br>If the student says all of the letter sounds correctly in the first row, but does not make any attempt to blend or recode, say **Try to read the words as whole words**.<br><br>If the student stops (and it's not a hesitation on a specific item), say **Keep going**. (Repeat as often as needed.)<br><br>If the student loses his/her place, point. (Repeat as often as needed.) |

NWF

sog mip

# 11 DIBELS® Nonsense Word Fluency
Progress Monitoring 11

**Directions:** Make sure you have reviewed the scoring rules in the *DIBELS Next Assessment Manual* and have them available. Say these specific directions to the student:

▶ *We are going to read some make-believe words. Listen. This word is "sog."* (Run your finger under the word as you say it.) *The sounds are /s/ /o/ /g/* (point to each letter). *Your turn. Read this make-believe word* (point to the word "mip"). *If you can't read the whole word, tell me any sounds you know.*

| | | |
|---|---|---|
| Correct Whole Word Read<br>mip | **Very good reading the word "mip."** | (Begin testing.) |
| Correct Letter Sounds<br>Any other response with all the correct letter sounds | **Very good. /m/ /i/ /p/** (point to each letter) **or "mip"** (run your finger under the word as you say it). | (Begin testing.) |

| | | | | |
|---|---|---|---|---|
| Incorrect response<br>No response within 3 <u>seconds</u>, or response includes any errors | **Listen. /m/ /i/ /p/ or "mip."** (Run your finger under the letters as you say the sounds.) **Your turn. Read this make-believe word.** (Point to the word "mip.") **If you can't read the whole word, tell me any sounds you know.** | Correct response | **Very good.** | (Begin testing.) |
| | | Incorrect response | **Okay.** | (Begin testing.) |

▶ **Begin testing.** *I would like you to read more make-believe words. Do your best reading. If you can't read the whole word, tell me any sounds you know.* Go to the next page.

NWF

| | | | | |
|---|---|---|---|---|
| ▶ pip | duv | ak | wot | lep |
| fuz | mek | yig | aj | nof |
| yuv | kot | yep | sim | laj |
| ec | nov | yag | tup | dib |
| uk | yek | hob | bik | sav |
| dof | zaz | del | hiz | jub |
| bod | av | zed | kiz | dul |
| fem | foz | yal | lis | ul |
| bem | pav | yiv | num | vom |
| yis | ap | tez | buf | pos |

▶ *Put your finger under the first word. Ready, begin.*

| | |
|---|---|
| **Timing** | 1 minute. Start your stopwatch after telling the student to begin. Place a bracket ( **]** ) and say **Stop** after 1 minute. |
| **Wait** | If the student responds sound-by-sound, mixes sounds and words, or sounds out and recodes, allow 3 seconds, then provide the correct letter sound.<br><br>If the student responds with whole words, allow 3 seconds, then provide the correct word. |
| **Discontinue** | If the student has no correct letter sounds in the first line, say **Stop** and record a score of 0. |
| **Reminders** | If the student does not read from left to right, say **Go this way**. (Sweep your finger across the row.) (Allowed one time.)<br><br>If the student says letter names, say **Say the sounds, not the letter names**. (Allowed one time.)<br><br>If the student reads the word first, then says the letter sounds, say **Just read the word**. (Allowed one time.)<br><br>If the student says all of the letter sounds correctly in the first row, but does not make any attempt to blend or recode, say **Try to read the words as whole words**.<br><br>If the student stops (and it's not a hesitation on a specific item), say **Keep going**. (Repeat as often as needed.)<br><br>If the student loses his/her place, point. (Repeat as often as needed.) |

NWF

sog mip

# 12 DIBELS® Nonsense Word Fluency
Progress Monitoring 12

**Directions:** Make sure you have reviewed the scoring rules in the *DIBELS Next Assessment Manual* and have them available. Say these specific directions to the student:

▶ *We are going to read some make-believe words. Listen. This word is* "sog." (Run your finger under the word as you say it.) *The sounds are /s/ /o/ /g/* (point to each letter). *Your turn. Read this make-believe word* (point to the word "mip"). *If you can't read the whole word, tell me any sounds you know.*

| | | |
|---|---|---|
| Correct Whole Word Read<br>mip | **Very good reading the word "mip."** | (Begin testing.) |

| | | |
|---|---|---|
| Correct Letter Sounds<br>Any other response with all the correct letter sounds | **Very good. /m/ /i/ /p/** (point to each letter) *or "mip"* (run your finger under the word as you say it). | (Begin testing.) |

| | | | | |
|---|---|---|---|---|
| Incorrect response<br>No response within 3 <u>seconds</u>, or response includes any errors | **Listen. /m/ /i/ /p/ or "mip."** (Run your finger under the letters as you say the sounds.) *Your turn. Read this make-believe word.* (Point to the word "mip.") *If you can't read the whole word, tell me any sounds you know.* | Correct response | **Very good.** | (Begin testing.) |
| | | Incorrect response | **Okay.** | (Begin testing.) |

▶ **Begin testing.** *I would like you to read more make-believe words. Do your best reading. If you can't read the whole word, tell me any sounds you know.* **Go to the next page.**

NWF

| | | | | |
|---|---|---|---|---|
| ▶ nid | tev | ab | wug | lon |
| boz | bak | zus | iv | nes |
| zuz | lif | yob | nec | kaj |
| ek | bov | yaf | dup | mib |
| od | jef | mif | fas | kuj |
| bab | yov | bub | fiz | vec |
| sed | ov | wuf | daj | rit |
| dak | loj | wum | kic | el |
| fac | lev | juj | hig | yon |
| jep | oc | lij | dal | lul |

# 12 DIBELS® Nonsense Word Fluency
Progress Monitoring 12 continued

▶ *Put your finger under the first word. Ready, begin.*

---

| | |
|---|---|
| *Timing* | 1 minute. Start your stopwatch after telling the student to begin. Place a bracket ( **]** ) and say ***Stop*** after 1 minute. |
| *Wait* | If the student responds sound-by-sound, mixes sounds and words, or sounds out and recodes, allow 3 seconds, then provide the correct letter sound. |
| | If the student responds with whole words, allow 3 seconds, then provide the correct word. |
| *Discontinue* | If the student has no correct letter sounds in the first line, say ***Stop*** and record a score of 0. |
| *Reminders* | If the student does not read from left to right, say ***Go this way***. (Sweep your finger across the row.) (Allowed one time.) |
| | If the student says letter names, say ***Say the sounds, not the letter names***. (Allowed one time.) |
| | If the student reads the word first, then says the letter sounds, say ***Just read the word***. (Allowed one time.) |
| | If the student says all of the letter sounds correctly in the first row, but does not make any attempt to blend or recode, say ***Try to read the words as whole words***. |
| | If the student stops (and it's not a hesitation on a specific item), say ***Keep going***. (Repeat as often as needed.) |
| | If the student loses his/her place, point. (Repeat as often as needed.) |

sog             mip

# 13 DIBELS® Nonsense Word Fluency
Progress Monitoring 13

*Directions:* Make sure you have reviewed the scoring rules in the *DIBELS Next Assessment Manual* and have them available. Say these specific directions to the student:

▶ *We are going to read some make-believe words. Listen. This word is "sog."* (Run your finger under the word as you say it.) *The sounds are /s/ /o/ /g/* (point to each letter). *Your turn. Read this make-believe word* (point to the word "mip"). *If you can't read the whole word, tell me any sounds you know.*

| | | |
|---|---|---|
| Correct Whole Word Read<br>mip | *Very good reading the word "mip."* | (Begin testing.) |

| | | |
|---|---|---|
| Correct Letter Sounds<br>Any other response with all the correct letter sounds | *Very good. /m/ /i/ /p/* (point to each letter) *or "mip"* (run your finger under the word as you say it). | (Begin testing.) |

| | | | | |
|---|---|---|---|---|
| Incorrect response<br>No response within 3 <u>seconds</u>, or response includes any errors | *Listen. /m/ /i/ /p/ or "mip."* (Run your finger under the letters as you say the sounds.) *Your turn. Read this make-believe word.* (Point to the word "mip.") *If you can't read the whole word, tell me any sounds you know.* | Correct response | *Very good.* | (Begin testing.) |
| | | Incorrect response | *Okay.* | (Begin testing.) |

▶ Begin testing. *I would like you to read more make-believe words. Do your best reading. If you can't read the whole word, tell me any sounds you know.* Go to the next page.

| | | | | |
|---|---|---|---|---|
| ▶ nug | bej | ol | zam | sig |
| kiv | som | ven | uz | kad |
| voz | fet | jud | mal | riv |
| im | sev | zop | tud | raf |
| ud | jel | pic | nac | boj |
| fil | woz | pas | suj | zeg |
| pol | av | vip | buv | sef |
| rec | biv | yom | fud | ac |
| kak | dov | zej | nul | yik |
| vek | af | nij | sot | mul |

▶ *Put your finger under the first word. Ready, begin.*

| | |
|---|---|
| **Timing** | 1 minute. Start your stopwatch after telling the student to begin. Place a bracket ( **]** ) and say **Stop** after 1 minute. |
| **Wait** | If the student responds sound-by-sound, mixes sounds and words, or sounds out and recodes, allow 3 seconds, then provide the correct letter sound. |
| | If the student responds with whole words, allow 3 seconds, then provide the correct word. |
| **Discontinue** | If the student has no correct letter sounds in the first line, say **Stop** and record a score of 0. |
| **Reminders** | If the student does not read from left to right, say **Go this way**. (Sweep your finger across the row.) (Allowed one time.) |
| | If the student says letter names, say **Say the sounds, not the letter names**. (Allowed one time.) |
| | If the student reads the word first, then says the letter sounds, say **Just read the word**. (Allowed one time.) |
| | If the student says all of the letter sounds correctly in the first row, but does not make any attempt to blend or recode, say **Try to read the words as whole words**. |
| | If the student stops (and it's not a hesitation on a specific item), say **Keep going**. (Repeat as often as needed.) |
| | If the student loses his/her place, point. (Repeat as often as needed.) |

NWF

sog          mip

# 14 DIBELS® Nonsense Word Fluency
Progress Monitoring 14

***Directions:*** Make sure you have reviewed the scoring rules in the *DIBELS Next Assessment Manual* and have them available. Say these specific directions to the student:

▶ ***We are going to read some make-believe words. Listen. This word is "sog."*** (Run your finger under the word as you say it.) ***The sounds are /s/ /o/ /g/*** (point to each letter). ***Your turn. Read this make-believe word*** (point to the word "mip"). ***If you can't read the whole word, tell me any sounds you know.***

| | | |
|---|---|---|
| *Correct Whole Word Read*<br>mip | ***Very good reading the word "mip."*** | (Begin testing.) |

| | | |
|---|---|---|
| *Correct Letter Sounds*<br>Any other response with all the correct letter sounds | ***Very good. /m/ /i/ /p/*** (point to each letter) ***or "mip"*** (run your finger under the word as you say it). | (Begin testing.) |

| | | | |
|---|---|---|---|
| *Incorrect response*<br>No response within 3 <u>seconds</u>, or response includes any errors | ***Listen. /m/ /i/ /p/ or "mip."*** (Run your finger under the letters as you say the sounds.) ***Your turn. Read this make-believe word.*** (Point to the word "mip.") ***If you can't read the whole word, tell me any sounds you know.*** | *Correct response* | ***Very good.*** (Begin testing.) |
| | | *Incorrect response* | ***Okay.*** (Begin testing.) |

▶ **Begin testing.** *I would like you to read more make-believe words. Do your best reading. If you can't read the whole word, tell me any sounds you know.* Go to the next page.

| ▶ mab | soz | uc | wec | ric |
|-------|-----|-----|-----|-----|
| suz | nic | veb | aj | moc |
| jiv | sul | wep | poc | tav |
| ob | mav | zud | leb | bif |
| eg | jup | dob | lic | dav |
| bip | wev | nal | foj | juk |
| pob | uv | yad | biz | tef |
| lok | kav | yul | pem | ik |
| tik | hov | wez | hud | wak |
| wek | um | fav | fos | ril |

▶ *Put your finger under the first word. Ready, begin.*

| | |
|---|---|
| **Timing** | 1 minute. Start your stopwatch after telling the student to begin. Place a bracket ( ] ) and say **Stop** after 1 minute. |
| **Wait** | If the student responds sound-by-sound, mixes sounds and words, or sounds out and recodes, allow 3 seconds, then provide the correct letter sound. |
| | If the student responds with whole words, allow 3 seconds, then provide the correct word. |
| **Discontinue** | If the student has no correct letter sounds in the first line, say **Stop** and record a score of 0. |
| **Reminders** | If the student does not read from left to right, say **Go this way**. (Sweep your finger across the row.) (Allowed one time.) |
| | If the student says letter names, say **Say the sounds, not the letter names**. (Allowed one time.) |
| | If the student reads the word first, then says the letter sounds, say **Just read the word**. (Allowed one time.) |
| | If the student says all of the letter sounds correctly in the first row, but does not make any attempt to blend or recode, say **Try to read the words as whole words**. |
| | If the student stops (and it's not a hesitation on a specific item), say **Keep going**. (Repeat as often as needed.) |
| | If the student loses his/her place, point. (Repeat as often as needed.) |

NWF

sog                    mip

# 15 DIBELS® Nonsense Word Fluency
Progress Monitoring 15

**Directions:** Make sure you have reviewed the scoring rules in the *DIBELS Next Assessment Manual* and have them available. Say these specific directions to the student:

▶ *We are going to read some make-believe words. Listen. This word is "sog."* (Run your finger under the word as you say it.) *The sounds are /s/ /o/ /g/* (point to each letter). *Your turn. Read this make-believe word* (point to the word "mip"). *If you can't read the whole word, tell me any sounds you know.*

| | | |
|---|---|---|
| *Correct Whole Word Read*<br>mip | *Very good reading the word "mip."* | (Begin testing.) |
| *Correct Letter Sounds*<br>Any other response with all the correct letter sounds | *Very good. /m/ /i/ /p/* (point to each letter) *or "mip"* (run your finger under the word as you say it)*.* | (Begin testing.) |

| | | | | |
|---|---|---|---|---|
| *Incorrect response*<br>No response within 3 <u>seconds</u>, or response includes any errors | *Listen. /m/ /i/ /p/ or "mip."* (Run your finger under the letters as you say the sounds.) *Your turn. Read this make-believe word.* (Point to the word "mip.") *If you can't read the whole word, tell me any sounds you know.* | *Correct response* | *Very good.* | (Begin testing.) |
| | | *Incorrect response* | *Okay.* | (Begin testing.) |

▶ **Begin testing.** *I would like you to read more make-believe words. Do your best reading. If you can't read the whole word, tell me any sounds you know.* **Go to the next page.**

| | | | | |
|---|---|---|---|---|
| ► tok | tiz | ep | vaf | dut |
| hej | sim | zuc | az | kos |
| vev | kan | wuk | fon | dij |
| ig | paj | jok | fel | kup |
| es | wil | mag | tob | kuz |
| pab | yev | sos | huj | zif |
| lat | ij | wef | fov | buk |
| pel | siv | zaf | nos | uf |
| hod | buj | yiz | ren | wan |
| wub | og | lav | bip | bek |

# 15 DIBELS® Nonsense Word Fluency
## Progress Monitoring 15 continued

▶ *Put your finger under the first word. Ready, begin.*

| | |
|---|---|
| **Timing** | 1 minute. Start your stopwatch after telling the student to begin. Place a bracket ( ] ) and say **Stop** after 1 minute. |
| **Wait** | If the student responds sound-by-sound, mixes sounds and words, or sounds out and recodes, allow 3 seconds, then provide the correct letter sound.<br><br>If the student responds with whole words, allow 3 seconds, then provide the correct word. |
| **Discontinue** | If the student has no correct letter sounds in the first line, say **Stop** and record a score of 0. |
| **Reminders** | If the student does not read from left to right, say **Go this way**. (Sweep your finger across the row.) (Allowed one time.)<br><br>If the student says letter names, say **Say the sounds, not the letter names**. (Allowed one time.)<br><br>If the student reads the word first, then says the letter sounds, say **Just read the word**. (Allowed one time.)<br><br>If the student says all of the letter sounds correctly in the first row, but does not make any attempt to blend or recode, say **Try to read the words as whole words**.<br><br>If the student stops (and it's not a hesitation on a specific item), say **Keep going**. (Repeat as often as needed.)<br><br>If the student loses his/her place, point. (Repeat as often as needed.) |

sog          mip

# 16 DIBELS® Nonsense Word Fluency
Progress Monitoring 16

***Directions:*** Make sure you have reviewed the scoring rules in the *DIBELS Next Assessment Manual* and have them available. Say these specific directions to the student:

▶ *We are going to read some make-believe words. Listen. This word is "sog."* (Run your finger under the word as you say it.) *The sounds are /s/ /o/ /g/* (point to each letter). *Your turn. Read this make-believe word* (point to the word "mip"). *If you can't read the whole word, tell me any sounds you know.*

| | | |
|---|---|---|
| *Correct Whole Word Read* <br> mip | ***Very good reading the word "mip."*** | (Begin testing.) |
| *Correct Letter Sounds* <br> Any other response with all the correct letter sounds | ***Very good. /m/ /i/ /p/*** (point to each letter) ***or "mip"*** (run your finger under the word as you say it). | (Begin testing.) |

| | | | | |
|---|---|---|---|---|
| *Incorrect response* <br> No response within 3 <u>seconds</u>, or response includes any errors | ***Listen. /m/ /i/ /p/ or "mip."*** (Run your finger under the letters as you say the sounds.) ***Your turn. Read this make-believe word.*** (Point to the word "mip.") ***If you can't read the whole word, tell me any sounds you know.*** | *Correct response* | ***Very good.*** | (Begin testing.) |
| | | *Incorrect response* | ***Okay.*** | (Begin testing.) |

▶ **Begin testing.** *I would like you to read more make-believe words. Do your best reading. If you can't read the whole word, tell me any sounds you know.* **Go to the next page.**

| | | | | |
|---|---|---|---|---|
| ▶ tik | tev | ot | wak | rul |
| poj | tig | yad | uj | feb |
| wuz | hoc | yil | taf | dev |
| eb | sij | wol | nan | kud |
| em | vup | fap | fid | moz |
| dit | joz | dem | taj | wup |
| tuk | oj | jed | mij | nak |
| mok | kev | vab | luk | id |
| fif | kez | wuv | nom | yas |
| jod | ug | hiv | kef | bap |

# 16 DIBELS® Nonsense Word Fluency
Progress Monitoring 16 continued

▶ *Put your finger under the first word. Ready, begin.*

| | |
|---|---|
| **Timing** | 1 minute. Start your stopwatch after telling the student to begin. Place a bracket ( **]** ) and say **Stop** after 1 minute. |
| **Wait** | If the student responds sound-by-sound, mixes sounds and words, or sounds out and recodes, allow 3 seconds, then provide the correct letter sound. |
| | If the student responds with whole words, allow 3 seconds, then provide the correct word. |
| **Discontinue** | If the student has no correct letter sounds in the first line, say **Stop** and record a score of 0. |
| **Reminders** | If the student does not read from left to right, say **Go this way**. (Sweep your finger across the row.) (Allowed one time.) |
| | If the student says letter names, say **Say the sounds, not the letter names**. (Allowed one time.) |
| | If the student reads the word first, then says the letter sounds, say **Just read the word**. (Allowed one time.) |
| | If the student says all of the letter sounds correctly in the first row, but does not make any attempt to blend or recode, say **Try to read the words as whole words**. |
| | If the student stops (and it's not a hesitation on a specific item), say **Keep going**. (Repeat as often as needed.) |
| | If the student loses his/her place, point. (Repeat as often as needed.) |

NWF

sog          mip

# 17 DIBELS® Nonsense Word Fluency
## Progress Monitoring 17

**Directions:** Make sure you have reviewed the scoring rules in the *DIBELS Next Assessment Manual* and have them available. Say these specific directions to the student:

▶ *We are going to read some make-believe words. Listen. This word is "sog."* (Run your finger under the word as you say it.) *The sounds are /s/ /o/ /g/* (point to each letter). *Your turn. Read this make-believe word* (point to the word "mip"). *If you can't read the whole word, tell me any sounds you know.*

| | | |
|---|---|---|
| Correct Whole Word Read<br>mip | **Very good reading the word "mip."** | (Begin testing.) |
| Correct Letter Sounds<br>Any other response with all the correct letter sounds | **Very good. /m/ /i/ /p/** (point to each letter) **or "mip"** (run your finger under the word as you say it)**.** | (Begin testing.) |

| | | | | |
|---|---|---|---|---|
| Incorrect response<br>No response within 3 <u>seconds</u>, or response includes any errors | **Listen. /m/ /i/ /p/ or "mip."** (Run your finger under the letters as you say the sounds.) **Your turn. Read this make-believe word.** (Point to the word "mip.") **If you can't read the whole word, tell me any sounds you know.** | Correct response | **Very good.** | (Begin testing.) |
| | | Incorrect response | **Okay.** | (Begin testing.) |

▶ **Begin testing.** *I would like you to read more make-believe words. Do your best reading. If you can't read the whole word, tell me any sounds you know.* Go to the next page.

| | | | | |
|---|---|---|---|---|
| ▶ kap | tuz | ib | yel | rof |
| naj | bul | yog | iv | fef |
| yov | huk | vil | rac | lej |
| ag | liv | jos | tes | hup |
| os | zas | tis | nuk | rev |
| pog | vuv | dap | tez | wis |
| daf | ev | zul | foz | til |
| kop | saj | zif | hul | ef |
| rek | raj | zuj | ros | zim |
| yan | ub | koj | min | fek |

# 17 DIBELS® Nonsense Word Fluency
Progress Monitoring 17 continued

▶ *Put your finger under the first word. Ready, begin.*

| Timing | 1 minute. Start your stopwatch after telling the student to begin. Place a bracket ( ] ) and say **Stop** after 1 minute. |
|---|---|
| Wait | If the student responds sound-by-sound, mixes sounds and words, or sounds out and recodes, allow 3 seconds, then provide the correct letter sound.<br><br>If the student responds with whole words, allow 3 seconds, then provide the correct word. |
| Discontinue | If the student has no correct letter sounds in the first line, say **Stop** and record a score of 0. |
| Reminders | If the student does not read from left to right, say **Go this way**. (Sweep your finger across the row.) (Allowed one time.)<br><br>If the student says letter names, say **Say the sounds, not the letter names**. (Allowed one time.)<br><br>If the student reads the word first, then says the letter sounds, say **Just read the word**. (Allowed one time.)<br><br>If the student says all of the letter sounds correctly in the first row, but does not make any attempt to blend or recode, say **Try to read the words as whole words**.<br><br>If the student stops (and it's not a hesitation on a specific item), say **Keep going**. (Repeat as often as needed.)<br><br>If the student loses his/her place, point. (Repeat as often as needed.) |

NWF

sog          mip

# 18 DIBELS® Nonsense Word Fluency
Progress Monitoring 18

*Directions:* Make sure you have reviewed the scoring rules in the *DIBELS Next Assessment Manual* and have them available. Say these specific directions to the student:

▶ *We are going to read some make-believe words. Listen. This word is "sog."* (Run your finger under the word as you say it.) *The sounds are /s/ /o/ /g/* (point to each letter). *Your turn. Read this make-believe word* (point to the word "mip"). *If you can't read the whole word, tell me any sounds you know.*

| | | |
|---|---|---|
| Correct Whole Word Read mip | *Very good reading the word "mip."* | (Begin testing.) |
| Correct Letter Sounds Any other response with all the correct letter sounds | *Very good. /m/ /i/ /p/* (point to each letter) *or "mip"* (run your finger under the word as you say it). | (Begin testing.) |

| | | | | |
|---|---|---|---|---|
| Incorrect response No response within 3 <u>seconds</u>, or response includes any errors | *Listen. /m/ /i/ /p/ or "mip."* (Run your finger under the letters as you say the sounds.) *Your turn. Read this make-believe word.* (Point to the word "mip.") *If you can't read the whole word, tell me any sounds you know.* | Correct response | *Very good.* | (Begin testing.) |
| | | Incorrect response | *Okay.* | (Begin testing.) |

▶ Begin testing. *I would like you to read more make-believe words. Do your best reading. If you can't read the whole word, tell me any sounds you know.* Go to the next page.

| | | | | |
|---|---|---|---|---|
| ▶ kot | nez | uf | val | hib |
| nav | tel | wif | ov | hup |
| yuv | kik | zep | nan | lov |
| em | miz | wod | rud | kak |
| og | yus | mak | teg | tij |
| tid | voz | fum | bav | yed |
| luf | aj | yib | hoz | pef |
| nom | suv | jek | dat | ic |
| rab | suz | vez | bos | yil |
| wen | ob | bij | fud | sal |

# 18 DIBELS® Nonsense Word Fluency
Progress Monitoring 18 continued

▶ *Put your finger under the first word. Ready, begin.*

| | |
|---|---|
| **Timing** | 1 minute. Start your stopwatch after telling the student to begin. Place a bracket ( **]** ) and say ***Stop*** after 1 minute. |
| **Wait** | If the student responds sound-by-sound, mixes sounds and words, or sounds out and recodes, allow 3 seconds, then provide the correct letter sound. |
| | If the student responds with whole words, allow 3 seconds, then provide the correct word. |
| **Discontinue** | If the student has no correct letter sounds in the first line, say ***Stop*** and record a score of 0. |
| **Reminders** | If the student does not read from left to right, say ***Go this way***. (Sweep your finger across the row.) (Allowed one time.) |
| | If the student says letter names, say ***Say the sounds, not the letter names***. (Allowed one time.) |
| | If the student reads the word first, then says the letter sounds, say ***Just read the word***. (Allowed one time.) |
| | If the student says all of the letter sounds correctly in the first row, but does not make any attempt to blend or recode, say ***Try to read the words as whole words***. |
| | If the student stops (and it's not a hesitation on a specific item), say ***Keep going***. (Repeat as often as needed.) |
| | If the student loses his/her place, point. (Repeat as often as needed.) |

NWF

sog             mip

# 19 DIBELS® Nonsense Word Fluency
Progress Monitoring 19

***Directions:*** Make sure you have reviewed the scoring rules in the *DIBELS Next Assessment Manual* and have them available. Say these specific directions to the student:

▶ ***We are going to read some make-believe words. Listen. This word is "sog."*** (Run your finger under the word as you say it.) ***The sounds are /s/ /o/ /g/*** (point to each letter). ***Your turn. Read this make-believe word*** (point to the word "mip"). ***If you can't read the whole word, tell me any sounds you know.***

| Correct Whole Word Read<br>mip | ***Very good reading the word "mip."*** | | (Begin testing.) | |
| --- | --- | --- | --- | --- |
| *Correct Letter Sounds*<br>Any other response with all the correct letter sounds | ***Very good. /m/ /i/ /p/*** (point to each letter) ***or "mip"*** (run your finger under the word as you say it)***.*** | | (Begin testing.) | |
| *Incorrect response*<br>No response within 3 <u>seconds</u>, or response includes any errors | ***Listen. /m/ /i/ /p/ or "mip."*** (Run your finger under the letters as you say the sounds.) ***Your turn. Read this make-believe word.*** (Point to the word "mip.") ***If you can't read the whole word, tell me any sounds you know.*** | *Correct response* | ***Very good.*** | (Begin testing.) |
| | | | *Incorrect response* | ***Okay.*** | (Begin testing.) |

▶ ***Begin testing. I would like you to read more make-believe words. Do your best reading. If you can't read the whole word, tell me any sounds you know.*** **Go to the next page.**

| | | | | |
|---|---|---|---|---|
| ► kup | tej | ab | woc | fis |
| huv | non | zed | ij | sak |
| zav | reb | yol | pik | luj |
| ac | pez | zuf | bik | mog |
| ec | wuf | nog | dak | siz |
| rep | yuz | fol | rav | jik |
| bef | oj | zil | fuz | faf |
| mos | fez | vis | pag | um |
| tak | buv | woj | hin | vec |
| vep | od | fuj | lil | laf |

▶ *Put your finger under the first word. Ready, begin.*

| Timing | 1 minute. Start your stopwatch after telling the student to begin. Place a bracket ( **]** ) and say **Stop** after 1 minute. |
|---|---|
| Wait | If the student responds sound-by-sound, mixes sounds and words, or sounds out and recodes, allow 3 seconds, then provide the correct letter sound.<br><br>If the student responds with whole words, allow 3 seconds, then provide the correct word. |
| Discontinue | If the student has no correct letter sounds in the first line, say **Stop** and record a score of 0. |
| Reminders | If the student does not read from left to right, say **Go this way**. (Sweep your finger across the row.) (Allowed one time.)<br><br>If the student says letter names, say **Say the sounds, not the letter names**. (Allowed one time.)<br><br>If the student reads the word first, then says the letter sounds, say **Just read the word**. (Allowed one time.)<br><br>If the student says all of the letter sounds correctly in the first row, but does not make any attempt to blend or recode, say **Try to read the words as whole words**.<br><br>If the student stops (and it's not a hesitation on a specific item), say **Keep going**. (Repeat as often as needed.)<br><br>If the student loses his/her place, point. (Repeat as often as needed.) |

NWF

sog          mip

# 20 DIBELS® Nonsense Word Fluency
Progress Monitoring 20

**Directions:** Make sure you have reviewed the scoring rules in the *DIBELS Next Assessment Manual* and have them available. Say these specific directions to the student:

► *We are going to read some make-believe words. Listen. This word is "sog."* (Run your finger under the word as you say it.) *The sounds are /s/ /o/ /g/* (point to each letter). *Your turn. Read this make-believe word* (point to the word "mip"). *If you can't read the whole word, tell me any sounds you know.*

| | | |
|---|---|---|
| Correct Whole Word Read<br>mip | **Very good reading the word "mip."** | (Begin testing.) |
| Correct Letter Sounds<br>Any other response with all the correct letter sounds | **Very good. /m/ /i/ /p/** (point to each letter) **or "mip"** (run your finger under the word as you say it). | (Begin testing.) |

| | | | | |
|---|---|---|---|---|
| Incorrect response<br>No response within 3 <u>seconds</u>, or response includes any errors | **Listen. /m/ /i/ /p/ or "mip."** (Run your finger under the letters as you say the sounds.) **Your turn. Read this make-believe word.** (Point to the word "mip.") **If you can't read the whole word, tell me any sounds you know.** | Correct response | **Very good.** | (Begin testing.) |
| | | Incorrect response | **Okay.** | (Begin testing.) |

► **Begin testing.** *I would like you to read more make-believe words. Do your best reading. If you can't read the whole word, tell me any sounds you know.* **Go to the next page.**

NWF

| | | | | |
|---|---|---|---|---|
| ▶ kek | fiv | os | zul | hal |
| luv | ras | jof | iv | peb |
| yiz | lus | yel | kam | toz |
| ub | sez | zod | fas | hil |
| ap | zup | heg | bif | moj |
| nic | yav | lud | nej | zog |
| nof | uv | zak | sej | bil |
| pim | dej | jun | lan | op |
| bas | tuv | wej | tog | wic |
| jem | ug | tiv | rog | kal |

▶ *Put your finger under the first word. Ready, begin.*

| | |
|---|---|
| **Timing** | 1 minute. Start your stopwatch after telling the student to begin. Place a bracket ( **]** ) and say **Stop** after 1 minute. |
| **Wait** | If the student responds sound-by-sound, mixes sounds and words, or sounds out and recodes, allow 3 seconds, then provide the correct letter sound. |
| | If the student responds with whole words, allow 3 seconds, then provide the correct word. |
| **Discontinue** | If the student has no correct letter sounds in the first line, say **Stop** and record a score of 0. |
| **Reminders** | If the student does not read from left to right, say **Go this way**. (Sweep your finger across the row.) (Allowed one time.) |
| | If the student says letter names, say **Say the sounds, not the letter names**. (Allowed one time.) |
| | If the student reads the word first, then says the letter sounds, say **Just read the word**. (Allowed one time.) |
| | If the student says all of the letter sounds correctly in the first row, but does not make any attempt to blend or recode, say **Try to read the words as whole words**. |
| | If the student stops (and it's not a hesitation on a specific item), say **Keep going**. (Repeat as often as needed.) |
| | If the student loses his/her place, point. (Repeat as often as needed.) |

NWF

## DIBELS® Oral Reading Fluency
Level 1/Progress Monitoring

***Directions:*** Make sure you have reviewed the scoring rules in the *DIBELS Next Assessment Manual* and have them available. Say these specific directions to the student:

---

▶ *I would like you to read a story to me. Please do your best reading. If you do not know a word, I will read the word for you. Keep reading until I say "stop." Be ready to tell me all about the story when you finish.*

▶ **Go to the next Progress Monitoring passage in the sequence.**

# A Busy Saturday

▶ The morning light filled the room. Mel jumped out of bed and put on her clothes. She had a busy Saturday planned. She could not wait to get started.

First, Mel and her mom made Mel's favorite food. Her mom cut a banana in half. Then Mel spread peanut butter on both sides. She brought the two pieces together and ate her banana sandwich outside in the sun.

Soon Mel's big brother came out with some chalk. They drew a line on the driveway. After putting on helmets, they skated along the line. Mel went very slowly. She was just learning to skate. Her brother helped her skate in a straight line and not fall down.

Now it was time for art. Mel went to the art box. Her mom often filled it with fun things. Mel got an idea when she saw some socks. She made a dog puppet and a bird puppet out of the socks. Then she wrote a play about them. She asked her brother and mom to come watch. They liked the show and clapped when it ended.

That night, Mel helped her mom make dinner. Then she read a book until it was time for bed. When Mel turned out the light, she thought about all the fun things she had done.

# 1 DIBELS® Oral Reading Fluency
Level 1/Progress Monitoring 1

Read the directions on page 83.

▶ **Begin testing.** *Put your finger under the first word* (point to the first word of the passage). *Ready, begin.*

---

| | |
|---|---|
| *Timing* | 1 minute. Start your stopwatch after the student says the first word of the passage. Place a bracket ( **]** ) and say *Stop* after 1 minute. |
| *Wait* | If no response in 3 seconds, say the word and mark it as incorrect. |
| *Discontinue* | If no words are read correctly in the first line, say *Stop*, record a score of 0, and do not administer Retell. |
| | If fewer than 40 words are read correctly on any passage, use professional judgment whether to administer Retell for that passage. |
| *Reminders* | If the student stops (and it's not a hesitation on a specific item), say *Keep going.* (Repeat as often as needed.) |
| | If the student loses her/his place, point. (Repeat as often as needed.) |

# 1 DIBELS® Oral Reading Fluency
Level 1/Progress Monitoring 1 Retell

▶ *Now tell me as much as you can about the story you just read. Ready, begin.*

| | |
|---|---|
| *Timing* | 1-minute maximum. Start your stopwatch after telling the student to begin. Say ***Stop*** after 1 minute. |
| *Wait/ Reminder* | If the student stops or hesitates for 3 seconds, select *one* of the following (allowed one time):<br>—If the student has not said anything at all, provides a very limited response, or provides an off-track response, say ***Tell me as much as you can about the story***.<br>—Otherwise, ask ***Can you tell me anything more about the story?*** |
| *Discontinue* | After the first reminder, if the student does not say anything or gets off track for 5 seconds, say ***Thank you*** and discontinue the task. |

## Tap Dance

▶ If you hear a song you like, you might tap your foot to the beat. Tapping the feet is a fun way to move to the music. It is no surprise that foot tapping turned into a dance. It is called tap dance. Tap dance has people use their feet to make sounds. The many sounds the feet make come together to form a kind of song. This makes it fun to watch and listen to tap.

Tap dancers wear special shoes with metal plates on the bottom. The plates are called taps. When the taps hit the floor they make noise. Dancers move their feet around to make different noises. The moves are called steps. Each step has a different name. Some common steps are the brush, stomp, and shuffle. When dancers first learn how to tap, they start slow. When they get better, their feet will move faster. They may also learn very hard steps. These take a long time to master.

Tap dance has been around for many years. Like many kinds of dance, it has changed over time. One great tap dance team called Slap and Happy added turns and even acrobatics. People became excited to watch tap. Soon, tap appeared on TV and in movies. Thanks to the many shows that use tap, this kind of dance is still enjoyed to this day.

# 2 DIBELS® Oral Reading Fluency
Level 1/Progress Monitoring 2

Read the directions on page 83.

▶ Begin testing. *Put your finger under the first word* (point to the first word of the passage). *Ready, begin.*

| | |
|---|---|
| *Timing* | 1 minute. Start your stopwatch after the student says the first word of the passage. Place a bracket ( **]** ) and say *Stop* after 1 minute. |
| *Wait* | If no response in 3 seconds, say the word and mark it as incorrect. |
| *Discontinue* | If no words are read correctly in the first line, say *Stop*, record a score of 0, and do not administer Retell.<br><br>If fewer than 40 words are read correctly on any passage, use professional judgment whether to administer Retell for that passage. |
| *Reminders* | If the student stops (and it's not a hesitation on a specific item), say *Keep going.* (Repeat as often as needed.)<br><br>If the student loses her/his place, point. (Repeat as often as needed.) |

# 2 DIBELS® Oral Reading Fluency
Level 1/Progress Monitoring 2 Retell

▶ *Now tell me as much as you can about the story you just read. Ready, begin.*

| | |
|---|---|
| *Timing* | 1-minute maximum. Start your stopwatch after telling the student to begin. Say ***Stop*** after 1 minute. |
| *Wait/ Reminder* | If the student stops or hesitates for 3 seconds, select *one* of the following (allowed one time):<br>—If the student has not said anything at all, provides a very limited response, or provides an off-track response, say ***Tell me as much as you can about the story***.<br>—Otherwise, ask ***Can you tell me anything more about the story?*** |
| *Discontinue* | After the first reminder, if the student does not say anything or gets off track for 5 seconds, say ***Thank you*** and discontinue the task. |

# The Yellow Snake

▶ Jane was so happy. Her class was going on a field trip to Reptile Gardens. There would be lots of snakes, lizards, and turtles. Some people do not like these kinds of animals, but Jane liked them best of all.

The first thing Jane and her class saw when they got to Reptile Gardens was a room filled with snakes. They were all different sizes and colors. Jane thought they were very pretty. She saw a worker holding a big snake. It was bright yellow. Jane had never seen a yellow snake before. The worker saw her watching and smiled at her.

"Would you like to see what the snake feels like?" she asked. Jane said yes and touched it gently. It was dry, smooth and cool. Jane grinned. This was great!

Next the class went to a room that was full of giant turtles. Jane watched them as they swam in the water. They were a lot bigger than the snakes. She liked to watch the turtles, and wanted to touch one. Her teacher said that was not a good idea.

All too soon it was time to go home. Jane was glad the Reptile Gardens were close by. She knew she would come back again to see the big yellow snake.

# 3 DIBELS® Oral Reading Fluency
Level 1/Progress Monitoring 3

Read the directions on page 83.

▶ **Begin testing. *Put your finger under the first word*** (point to the first word of the passage). ***Ready, begin.***

| | |
|---|---|
| *Timing* | 1 minute. Start your stopwatch after the student says the first word of the passage. Place a bracket ( **]** ) and say ***Stop*** after 1 minute. |
| *Wait* | If no response in 3 seconds, say the word and mark it as incorrect. |
| *Discontinue* | If no words are read correctly in the first line, say ***Stop***, record a score of 0, and do not administer Retell. |
| | If fewer than 40 words are read correctly on any passage, use professional judgment whether to administer Retell for that passage. |
| *Reminders* | If the student stops (and it's not a hesitation on a specific item), say ***Keep going.*** (Repeat as often as needed.) |
| | If the student loses her/his place, point. (Repeat as often as needed.) |

**3** **DIBELS® Oral Reading Fluency**
Level 1/Progress Monitoring 3 Retell

▶ *Now tell me as much as you can about the story you just read. Ready, begin.*

| | |
|---|---|
| *Timing* | 1-minute maximum. Start your stopwatch after telling the student to begin. Say *Stop* after 1 minute. |
| *Wait/ Reminder* | If the student stops or hesitates for 3 seconds, select *one* of the following (allowed one time):<br>—If the student has not said anything at all, provides a very limited response, or provides an off-track response, say *Tell me as much as you can about the story*.<br>—Otherwise, ask *Can you tell me anything more about the story?* |
| *Discontinue* | After the first reminder, if the student does not say anything or gets off track for 5 seconds, say *Thank you* and discontinue the task. |

# A Pancake Breakfast

▶ On a school day, the morning can be very busy. Most people eat breakfast foods that do not take much time to make. They might have cereal and milk or fruit with wheat toast. On the weekend, people are not in a rush. They can eat foods that take longer to fix. You might like to try cooking pancakes when you have the time.

To make pancakes, first you make the batter. Some people use a mix that they buy from the store. They add eggs and milk. Other people do not use a mix. They put flour, salt, and sugar in a bowl. Then they add the eggs and milk. All these things together make the batter. Stir the batter just a little bit. Too much stirring will make the pancakes heavy.

Next, heat a big flat pan, and pour some batter into the pan. Bubbles pop up, which make the pancakes get big. The bubbles are filled with air. The air makes the pancakes light and fluffy.

Soon, the pancakes turn brown around the sides. It is time to turn them over. They cook for a few more minutes. Then the cook puts all the pancakes on a plate.

Now it is time to add something on top. Some people like syrup. Others like fruits, such as strawberries. There are lots of things you can put on pancakes. Adding the topping is the last step. Now you can eat your tasty pancakes.

# 4 DIBELS® Oral Reading Fluency
Level 1/Progress Monitoring 4

Read the directions on page 83.

▶ **Begin testing.** *Put your finger under the first word* (point to the first word of the passage). *Ready, begin.*

| | |
|---|---|
| *Timing* | 1 minute. Start your stopwatch after the student says the first word of the passage. Place a bracket ( **]** ) and say *Stop* after 1 minute. |
| *Wait* | If no response in 3 seconds, say the word and mark it as incorrect. |
| *Discontinue* | If no words are read correctly in the first line, say *Stop*, record a score of 0, and do not administer Retell. |
| | If fewer than 40 words are read correctly on any passage, use professional judgment whether to administer Retell for that passage. |
| *Reminders* | If the student stops (and it's not a hesitation on a specific item), say *Keep going.* (Repeat as often as needed.) |
| | If the student loses her/his place, point. (Repeat as often as needed.) |

DORF/Level 1

# 4 DIBELS® Oral Reading Fluency
Level 1/Progress Monitoring 4 Retell

▶ *Now tell me as much as you can about the story you just read. Ready, begin.*

| | |
|---|---|
| **Timing** | 1-minute maximum. Start your stopwatch after telling the student to begin. Say **Stop** after 1 minute. |
| **Wait/ Reminder** | If the student stops or hesitates for 3 seconds, select *one* of the following (allowed one time):<br>—If the student has not said anything at all, provides a very limited response, or provides an off-track response, say **Tell me as much as you can about the story**.<br>—Otherwise, ask **Can you tell me anything more about the story?** |
| **Discontinue** | After the first reminder, if the student does not say anything or gets off track for 5 seconds, say **Thank you** and discontinue the task. |

DORF/Level 1

## Picking Apples

▶ The apple farm was having a picking party. Ren and her family had come to enjoy the fun. Ren could see a hayride and a man painting faces. There was even a woman juggling five apples above her head.

Ren wanted to pick apples first. She ran to the nearest tree. Smiling, Ren pulled off a big red apple. She opened her mouth wide. Crunch! As she took a bite, sweet juice ran down her chin. Ren quickly ate the apple. Now it was time to get to work. Ren filled her basket so she would have lots of apples to eat at home.

After picking red apples, Ren went to a tree that had green apples. These apples were not very sweet, but they made tasty pies and cakes. Ren got another basket. She picked as many apples as she could. When she tried to lift the basket, Ren could not pick it up. It was too heavy. Ren's mother smiled and asked her to get a wagon. Together, they put both of their baskets on the wagon and pulled it to their car.

The important work was done. Now Ren was ready to have fun. She went to get her face painted. Ren looked at all the pictures. Then she saw the one she wanted. When the man was done painting, Ren had a big red apple on her cheek.

# 5 DIBELS® Oral Reading Fluency
Level 1/Progress Monitoring 5

Read the directions on page 83.

▶ **Begin testing.** *Put your finger under the first word* (point to the first word of the passage). *Ready, begin.*

| | |
|---|---|
| *Timing* | 1 minute. Start your stopwatch after the student says the first word of the passage. Place a bracket ( **]** ) and say *Stop* after 1 minute. |
| *Wait* | If no response in 3 seconds, say the word and mark it as incorrect. |
| *Discontinue* | If no words are read correctly in the first line, say *Stop*, record a score of 0, and do not administer Retell. |
| | If fewer than 40 words are read correctly on any passage, use professional judgment whether to administer Retell for that passage. |
| *Reminders* | If the student stops (and it's not a hesitation on a specific item), say *Keep going.* (Repeat as often as needed.) |
| | If the student loses her/his place, point. (Repeat as often as needed.) |

# 5 DIBELS® Oral Reading Fluency
Level 1/Progress Monitoring 5 Retell

▶ *Now tell me as much as you can about the story you just read. Ready, begin.*

| | |
|---|---|
| **Timing** | 1-minute maximum. Start your stopwatch after telling the student to begin. Say **Stop** after 1 minute. |
| **Wait/ Reminder** | If the student stops or hesitates for 3 seconds, select *one* of the following (allowed one time):<br>—If the student has not said anything at all, provides a very limited response, or provides an off-track response, say **Tell me as much as you can about the story**.<br>—Otherwise, ask **Can you tell me anything more about the story?** |
| **Discontinue** | After the first reminder, if the student does not say anything or gets off track for 5 seconds, say **Thank you** and discontinue the task. |

# The Puppet Show

▶ Our class took a trip to the public library to see a puppet show. Students from other schools were there, too. The puppet show was in a special part of the library where there were books and chairs just for children. A lady read the story while the puppets performed the story. Our class had so much fun! We asked our teacher if we could make a puppet show of our own and she said yes.

When we got back to school we talked about ideas for a show. We raised our hands to share ideas. We each waited our turn while our teacher wrote the ideas on the white board. We talked about all of the ideas. Then we voted for the best one. The class voted to make the show about a trip to the library.

Our class made puppets out of socks and paper bags. Some of the puppets looked very silly. Mine had brown hair and red lips. Everyone had a job to do. Some children planned what the puppets would say. Other children made a stage out of a big box. We practiced the show over and over. Then we did our puppet show for the children in preschool. They loved it.

# 6 DIBELS® Oral Reading Fluency
Level 1/Progress Monitoring 6

Read the directions on page 83.

▶ **Begin testing.** *Put your finger under the first word* (point to the first word of the passage). *Ready, begin.*

| | |
|---|---|
| *Timing* | 1 minute. Start your stopwatch after the student says the first word of the passage. Place a bracket ( **]** ) and say *Stop* after 1 minute. |
| *Wait* | If no response in 3 seconds, say the word and mark it as incorrect. |
| *Discontinue* | If no words are read correctly in the first line, say *Stop*, record a score of 0, and do not administer Retell. |
| | If fewer than 40 words are read correctly on any passage, use professional judgment whether to administer Retell for that passage. |
| *Reminders* | If the student stops (and it's not a hesitation on a specific item), say *Keep going.* (Repeat as often as needed.) |
| | If the student loses her/his place, point. (Repeat as often as needed.) |

# 6 DIBELS® Oral Reading Fluency
Level 1/Progress Monitoring 6 Retell

▶ *Now tell me as much as you can about the story you just read. Ready, begin.*

| | |
|---|---|
| **Timing** | 1-minute maximum. Start your stopwatch after telling the student to begin. Say **Stop** after 1 minute. |
| **Wait/ Reminder** | If the student stops or hesitates for 3 seconds, select *one* of the following (allowed one time):<br>—If the student has not said anything at all, provides a very limited response, or provides an off-track response, say **Tell me as much as you can about the story**.<br>—Otherwise, ask **Can you tell me anything more about the story?** |
| **Discontinue** | After the first reminder, if the student does not say anything or gets off track for 5 seconds, say **Thank you** and discontinue the task. |

# Puzzles

▶ Do you like to solve puzzles? They can be a lot of fun. There are many kinds of puzzles. For many people, the puzzle they like best is a jigsaw puzzle. In a jigsaw puzzle, you make a picture out of many small pieces.

The first jigsaw puzzle was made by a map maker. First he made a map of the world. Then he cut around each nation. People had to try to put the pieces in the right place. Schools used this kind of puzzle to teach students where each nation of the world was located. It made learning about the world fun.

Next, a new kind of saw let puzzle makers cut puzzles into many small pieces. The pieces were often cut into odd shapes. Many more jigsaw puzzles were made. Then, they began to put fun pictures on them. People wanted to see what the picture would look like when it was done.

Today, you can buy many kinds of jigsaw puzzles. The hard ones have lots of tiny pieces. Some have pictures on both sides. Some are shaped like ships or castles. Some even have clues hidden in the picture. Then you get to solve a picture puzzle and a mystery.

# 7 DIBELS® Oral Reading Fluency
Level 1/Progress Monitoring 7

Read the directions on page 83.

▶ **Begin testing. *Put your finger under the first word*** (point to the first word of the passage). ***Ready, begin.***

---

| | |
|---|---|
| *Timing* | 1 minute. Start your stopwatch after the student says the first word of the passage. Place a bracket ( **]** ) and say ***Stop*** after 1 minute. |
| *Wait* | If no response in 3 seconds, say the word and mark it as incorrect. |
| *Discontinue* | If no words are read correctly in the first line, say ***Stop***, record a score of 0, and do not administer Retell. |
| | If fewer than 40 words are read correctly on any passage, use professional judgment whether to administer Retell for that passage. |
| *Reminders* | If the student stops (and it's not a hesitation on a specific item), say ***Keep going.*** (Repeat as often as needed.) |
| | If the student loses her/his place, point. (Repeat as often as needed.) |

# 7 DIBELS® Oral Reading Fluency
Level 1/Progress Monitoring 7 Retell

▶ *Now tell me as much as you can about the story you just read. Ready, begin.*

| Timing | 1-minute maximum. Start your stopwatch after telling the student to begin. Say **Stop** after 1 minute. |
|---|---|
| **Wait/ Reminder** | If the student stops or hesitates for 3 seconds, select *one* of the following (allowed one time):<br>—If the student has not said anything at all, provides a very limited response, or provides an off-track response, say **Tell me as much as you can about the story**.<br>—Otherwise, ask **Can you tell me anything more about the story?** |
| **Discontinue** | After the first reminder, if the student does not say anything or gets off track for 5 seconds, say **Thank you** and discontinue the task. |

# A Night at Grandma's House

▶ The car drove out the farm gate. Jon waved goodbye to his dad. Then he smiled at his grandma. He had been waiting all week to come spend the night with her. They always had so much fun together.

First, Jon and his grandma fed the animals. He threw corn to the chickens and feed cubes to the cows. Then he gave hay and water to the goats.

"This animal is hungry now," said Jon, pointing to himself.

Grandma made macaroni and cheese for dinner. After eating, Jon went to the orange room to play. It had been his father's room long ago. Jon got out some small cars and made a road of blocks to drive them on.

Grandma soon told Jon it was time for bed. He went to get his pajamas and bear out of his bag. Surprised, Jon found that he had left his bear at home. He wondered how he would be able to sleep.

Grandma thought for a minute. Then she opened the closet and pulled out a white box. Jon saw a brown bear with a flat nose inside. Grandma explained that Jon's father had slept with the bear when he was young. The nose was flat because Jon's father had used it as a pillow.

Jon held the bear close. Now he could go to sleep.

# 8 DIBELS® Oral Reading Fluency
Level 1/Progress Monitoring 8

Read the directions on page 83.

▶ **Begin testing. *Put your finger under the first word*** (point to the first word of the passage). ***Ready, begin.***

| | |
|---|---|
| *Timing* | 1 minute. Start your stopwatch after the student says the first word of the passage. Place a bracket ( **]** ) and say ***Stop*** after 1 minute. |
| *Wait* | If no response in 3 seconds, say the word and mark it as incorrect. |
| *Discontinue* | If no words are read correctly in the first line, say ***Stop***, record a score of 0, and do not administer Retell.<br><br>If fewer than 40 words are read correctly on any passage, use professional judgment whether to administer Retell for that passage. |
| *Reminders* | If the student stops (and it's not a hesitation on a specific item), say ***Keep going.*** (Repeat as often as needed.)<br><br>If the student loses her/his place, point. (Repeat as often as needed.) |

# 8 DIBELS® Oral Reading Fluency
Level 1/Progress Monitoring 8 Retell

▶ *Now tell me as much as you can about the story you just read. Ready, begin.*

| | |
|---|---|
| **Timing** | 1-minute maximum. Start your stopwatch after telling the student to begin. Say **Stop** after 1 minute. |
| **Wait/ Reminder** | If the student stops or hesitates for 3 seconds, select *one* of the following (allowed one time):<br>—If the student has not said anything at all, provides a very limited response, or provides an off-track response, say **Tell me as much as you can about the story**.<br>—Otherwise, ask **Can you tell me anything more about the story?** |
| **Discontinue** | After the first reminder, if the student does not say anything or gets off track for 5 seconds, say **Thank you** and discontinue the task. |

# Go to Sleep

▶ What do you do before you go to bed at night? You may read, play, or listen to a story. Then your mouth opens wide and you take in a big breath. You are yawning. That means it is time to go to sleep.

Sleep is a time when the body gets to rest. You are not playing or working. Most children sleep nine to twelve hours each night. The long resting time lets your body build up energy. Then you can work and play the next day.

When you sleep, your body changes. The beat of your heart slows. You do not breathe as fast. These changes help your body rest and relax so it can grow. During this time your body also works to fix places that are hurt or sick.

Sleep helps your mind, too. It lets your brain rest. The next day you are able to remember things more easily. Sleep can also help your brain solve problems.

As you can see, sleep is very important. It helps keep your body and mind healthy. The next time you yawn or feel tired, remember that your body may be telling you it needs to go to sleep.

# 9 DIBELS® Oral Reading Fluency
Level 1/Progress Monitoring 9

Read the directions on page 83.

▶ **Begin testing. *Put your finger under the first word*** (point to the first word of the passage). ***Ready, begin.***

| | |
|---|---|
| *Timing* | 1 minute. Start your stopwatch after the student says the first word of the passage. Place a bracket ( **]** ) and say ***Stop*** after 1 minute. |
| *Wait* | If no response in 3 seconds, say the word and mark it as incorrect. |
| *Discontinue* | If no words are read correctly in the first line, say ***Stop***, record a score of 0, and do not administer Retell. |
| | If fewer than 40 words are read correctly on any passage, use professional judgment whether to administer Retell for that passage. |
| *Reminders* | If the student stops (and it's not a hesitation on a specific item), say ***Keep going.*** (Repeat as often as needed.) |
| | If the student loses her/his place, point. (Repeat as often as needed.) |

# 9 DIBELS® Oral Reading Fluency
Level 1/Progress Monitoring 9 Retell

▶ *Now tell me as much as you can about the story you just read. Ready, begin.*

| | |
|---|---|
| *Timing* | 1-minute maximum. Start your stopwatch after telling the student to begin. Say **Stop** after 1 minute. |
| *Wait/ Reminder* | If the student stops or hesitates for 3 seconds, select *one* of the following (allowed one time):<br>—If the student has not said anything at all, provides a very limited response, or provides an off-track response, say **Tell me as much as you can about the story**.<br>—Otherwise, ask **Can you tell me anything more about the story?** |
| *Discontinue* | After the first reminder, if the student does not say anything or gets off track for 5 seconds, say **Thank you** and discontinue the task. |

## Shape Art

▶ It was time for art. The teacher told the children that spring had come. He asked them to draw a picture of something that showed the season.

Jed put his hands in his lap. He did not think he knew how to draw. The teacher asked Jed what was wrong.

"I am not good at drawing," Jed said.

"Think of everything you see as a group of shapes," said the teacher. "A house has a square wall and a triangle roof. Just draw the shapes."

Jed looked out the window. He saw a tree that was just starting to grow new leaves. He looked at the tree to find shapes.

First, Jed drew a long brown rectangle for the trunk. He drew more thin rectangles at the top of the trunk to make branches.

Which shape could Jed use to make the leaves? He looked out the window again. Jed drew some green ovals on the branches.

Jed had placed the tree in the middle of the paper. He thought it looked funny. So Jed made a line under the trunk to show the ground. Now the tree needed roots. He drew long thin triangles at the bottom of the trunk.

Something was still missing from Jed's picture. He looked out the

# 10 DIBELS® Oral Reading Fluency
Level 1/Progress Monitoring 10

Read the directions on page 83.

▶ **Begin testing.** *Put your finger under the first word* (point to the first word of the passage). *Ready, begin.*

| | |
|---|---|
| **Timing** | 1 minute. Start your stopwatch after the student says the first word of the passage. Place a bracket ( **]** ) and say *Stop* after 1 minute. |
| **Wait** | If no response in 3 seconds, say the word and mark it as incorrect. |
| **Discontinue** | If no words are read correctly in the first line, say *Stop*, record a score of 0, and do not administer Retell.<br><br>If fewer than 40 words are read correctly on any passage, use professional judgment whether to administer Retell for that passage. |
| **Reminders** | If the student stops (and it's not a hesitation on a specific item), say *Keep going.* (Repeat as often as needed.)<br>If the student loses her/his place, point. (Repeat as often as needed.) |
| **Turn page** | If student reaches the end of the page (designated by triangles in the scoring booklet) before the minute is up, turn the page and continue on the next page. Otherwise, proceed to Retell when the minute is up. |

## Shape Art

window and saw a red bird. Now Jed knew just what his tree needed. He drew a red bird with ovals for the head and body. Triangles made the bill and wings. Jed titled his picture, "Spring tree."

DORF/Level 1

# 10 DIBELS® Oral Reading Fluency
Level 1/Progress Monitoring 10

▶ *Now tell me as much as you can about the story you just read. Ready, begin.*

| | |
|---|---|
| **Timing** | 1-minute maximum. Start your stopwatch after telling the student to begin. Say **Stop** after 1 minute. |
| **Wait/ Reminder** | If the student stops or hesitates for 3 seconds, select *one* of the following (allowed one time):<br>—If the student has not said anything at all, provides a very limited response, or provides an off-track response, say **Tell me as much as you can about the story**.<br>—Otherwise, ask **Can you tell me anything more about the story?** |
| **Discontinue** | After the first reminder, if the student does not say anything or gets off track for 5 seconds, say **Thank you** and discontinue the task. |

# Watch Them Change and Grow

▶ "I see one," said Grandfather. "Put the net in the water and scoop him up before he gets away!"

Jill waited for the tadpole to swim close to the bank so that she could reach him. Quickly, she leaned over and caught the little creature in her net. She stared at it and watched it wriggle.

"He will grow and change into a fine frog," her grandfather said.

"I want to keep him and see him change," she said.

Grandfather told Jill that she could keep him. "But, when he grows into a frog, we'll have to bring him back to the creek."

Jill and her grandfather made a home with a fish tank. They put rocks at the bottom. Water plants added food and color. Next, they filled the tank with a little bit of water. Jill watched her tadpole change over the next few weeks. First, he grew back legs, then he grew front legs. His tail became smaller and smaller each day. Jill charted his growth.

One day it was clear that her pet had become a frog. It was time for him to go back to the creek. Jill and her grandfather took him back and set him free. The frog jumped away happily.

Jill grinned from ear to ear. "That's a fine frog," she said.

"Well, would you look at this?" said Grandfather.

# 11 DIBELS® Oral Reading Fluency
Level 1/Progress Monitoring 11 continued

Read the directions on page 83.

▶ **Begin testing. *Put your finger under the first word*** (point to the first word of the passage)*. **Ready, begin.***

| | |
|---|---|
| *Timing* | 1 minute. Start your stopwatch after the student says the first word of the passage. Place a bracket ( **]** ) and say ***Stop*** after 1 minute. |
| *Wait* | If no response in 3 seconds, say the word and mark it as incorrect. |
| *Discontinue* | If no words are read correctly in the first line, say ***Stop***, record a score of 0, and do not administer Retell. |
| | If fewer than 40 words are read correctly on any passage, use professional judgment whether to administer Retell for that passage. |
| *Reminders* | If the student stops (and it's not a hesitation on a specific item), say ***Keep going.*** (Repeat as often as needed.) |
| | If the student loses her/his place, point. (Repeat as often as needed.) |
| *Turn page* | If student reaches the end of the page (designated by triangles in the scoring booklet) before the minute is up, turn the page and continue on the next page. Otherwise, proceed to Retell when the minute is up. |

## Watch Them Change and Grow

"A caterpillar!" Jill replied. "Can I keep him? I want to see him change and grow!"

_____

DORF/Level 1

# 11 DIBELS® Oral Reading Fluency
Level 1/Progress Monitoring 11 Retell

▶ *Now tell me as much as you can about the story you just read. Ready, begin.*

| Timing | 1-minute maximum. Start your stopwatch after telling the student to begin. Say **Stop** after 1 minute. |
| --- | --- |
| **Wait/ Reminder** | If the student stops or hesitates for 3 seconds, select *one* of the following (allowed one time):<br>—If the student has not said anything at all, provides a very limited response, or provides an off-track response, say **Tell me as much as you can about the story**.<br>—Otherwise, ask **Can you tell me anything more about the story?** |
| **Discontinue** | After the first reminder, if the student does not say anything or gets off track for 5 seconds, say **Thank you** and discontinue the task. |

# Clams

▶ A clam is an animal that lives in the sea. A clam has two hard shells that cover a soft white body. A muscle holds the two shells together so they can open like a door. It helps open and close the clam shell. The clam opens the shell to eat. It closes the shell to be safe.

You may have never seen a clam. That is because they live buried in the sand of the ocean floor. Clams hide in the sand for safety. They have one foot, which they use to dig a hole in the sand. It is not like your foot. It is all one piece and does not have toes. The foot digs a hole by moving back and forth. The clam digs about two inches into the sand. Clams often stay in this hole their whole life.

To eat, clams push two tubes through the sand. One tube pulls in water and food. The other pushes out waste.

Sea otters eat clams if they can find them. They swim down to the ocean floor and dig in the sand for clams. Then the otter swims back up to the surface. Finally, the otter uses a rock to crack open the hard shell.

Most clams grow to be one to three inches long. Some grow to more than five feet long. These giant clams weigh up to 500 pounds. An otter would have a hard time eating a clam that big!

# 12 DIBELS® Oral Reading Fluency
Level 1/Progress Monitoring 12

Read the directions on page 83.

▶ **Begin testing. *Put your finger under the first word*** (point to the first word of the passage). ***Ready, begin.***

| | |
|---|---|
| *Timing* | 1 minute. Start your stopwatch after the student says the first word of the passage. Place a bracket ( **]** ) and say ***Stop*** after 1 minute. |
| *Wait* | If no response in 3 seconds, say the word and mark it as incorrect. |
| *Discontinue* | If no words are read correctly in the first line, say ***Stop***, record a score of 0, and do not administer Retell. |
| | If fewer than 40 words are read correctly on any passage, use professional judgment whether to administer Retell for that passage. |
| *Reminders* | If the student stops (and it's not a hesitation on a specific item), say ***Keep going.*** (Repeat as often as needed.) |
| | If the student loses her/his place, point. (Repeat as often as needed.) |

# 12 DIBELS® Oral Reading Fluency
Level 1/Progress Monitoring 12 Retell

▶ *Now tell me as much as you can about the story you just read. Ready, begin.*

| | |
|---|---|
| **Timing** | 1-minute maximum. Start your stopwatch after telling the student to begin. Say **Stop** after 1 minute. |
| **Wait/ Reminder** | If the student stops or hesitates for 3 seconds, select *one* of the following (allowed one time):<br><br>—If the student has not said anything at all, provides a very limited response, or provides an off-track response, say **Tell me as much as you can about the story**.<br><br>—Otherwise, ask **Can you tell me anything more about the story?** |
| **Discontinue** | After the first reminder, if the student does not say anything or gets off track for 5 seconds, say **Thank you** and discontinue the task. |

# The Talking Stone

▶ The teacher gathered the students into a circle. He held up a white stone in his hand.

"This is a talking stone," he told his students. "It helps us take turns so everyone has a chance to talk and a chance to listen. If we all speak at once, no one can hear. We can use the stone to help us. If you have the stone, it is your time to talk. If you do not have the stone, it is your time to listen. This way we can share, and everyone can hear."

Then the teacher asked the students to share something special they had done that day.

Jen raised her hand quickly. She wanted to share something that no one else would share. She wanted to talk about feeding the lizard. When the teacher passed the stone to another child, Jen put her hand down. It was her turn to listen.

The stone moved slowly. One girl talked about drawing pictures in art. Another boy talked about counting seeds in math. No one talked about the lizard.

Soon Tom held the stone. He sat beside Jen. Tom pointed to the lizard and told how he helped feed it. Then he passed the stone to Jen.

Jen took the stone. She could not think of anything special to say.

# 13 DIBELS® Oral Reading Fluency
Level 1/Progress Monitoring 13

Read the directions on page 83.

▶ **Begin testing.** *Put your finger under the first word* (point to the first word of the passage). *Ready, begin.*

---

| | |
|---|---|
| *Timing* | 1 minute. Start your stopwatch after the student says the first word of the passage. Place a bracket ( **]** ) and say *Stop* after 1 minute. |
| *Wait* | If no response in 3 seconds, say the word and mark it as incorrect. |
| *Discontinue* | If no words are read correctly in the first line, say *Stop*, record a score of 0, and do not administer Retell.<br><br>If fewer than 40 words are read correctly on any passage, use professional judgment whether to administer Retell for that passage. |
| *Reminders* | If the student stops (and it's not a hesitation on a specific item), say *Keep going.* (Repeat as often as needed.)<br><br>If the student loses her/his place, point. (Repeat as often as needed.) |
| *Turn page* | If student reaches the end of the page (designated by triangles in the scoring booklet) before the minute is up, turn the page and continue on the next page. Otherwise, proceed to Retell when the minute is up. |

## The Talking Stone

Jen looked at the stone. Then she knew what to say.

"I liked passing the talking stone," Jen said. "It helped me remember all the fun things we did today."

DORF/Level 1

# 13 DIBELS® Oral Reading Fluency
Level 1/Progress Monitoring 13 Retell

▶ *Now tell me as much as you can about the story you just read. Ready, begin.*

| | |
|---|---|
| *Timing* | 1-minute maximum. Start your stopwatch after telling the student to begin. Say **Stop** after 1 minute. |
| *Wait/ Reminder* | If the student stops or hesitates for 3 seconds, select *one* of the following (allowed one time):<br>—If the student has not said anything at all, provides a very limited response, or provides an off-track response, say **Tell me as much as you can about the story**.<br>—Otherwise, ask **Can you tell me anything more about the story?** |
| *Discontinue* | After the first reminder, if the student does not say anything or gets off track for 5 seconds, say **Thank you** and discontinue the task. |

## The Kite Contest

▶ It was kite day at the local park. Everyone Jim knew had a kite to fly. Jim had made the kite he would use. It was shaped like a triangle. He had painted an eagle on it. He knew that an eagle was a bird that flew very high. He hoped that his kite would fly high, too.

When Jim and his dad got to the park, Jim lifted his kite up. He felt the tug on the line and let the string out. The wind pulled the kite higher and higher. Before long, most of the string was gone. Jim saw that the end was not tied to the tube.

He tried to grab the string before the kite got away. Suddenly, a gust of wind yanked the string right out of his hand. The kite was flying away! Jim chased after it, trying to grab the loose string.

When the kite sailed over a tree, the string got caught on one of the branches. Happily, Jim saw that the kite kept bobbing in the wind. He would be able to save his kite after all.

A man walked over to Jim. "We've never had a tree fly a kite," he said. "You get the prize for finding a special way to fly a kite." The man gave Jim a prize!

Jim's dad reached up and grabbed the string. The kite came loose. Jim tied the string to the tube. He didn't want to lose his kite again.

# 14 DIBELS® Oral Reading Fluency
Level 1/Progress Monitoring 14

Read the directions on page 83.

▶ **Begin testing.** *Put your finger under the first word* (point to the first word of the passage). *Ready, begin.*

| | |
|---|---|
| *Timing* | 1 minute. Start your stopwatch after the student says the first word of the passage. Place a bracket ( **]** ) and say *Stop* after 1 minute. |
| *Wait* | If no response in 3 seconds, say the word and mark it as incorrect. |
| *Discontinue* | If no words are read correctly in the first line, say *Stop*, record a score of 0, and do not administer Retell. |
| | If fewer than 40 words are read correctly on any passage, use professional judgment whether to administer Retell for that passage. |
| *Reminders* | If the student stops (and it's not a hesitation on a specific item), say *Keep going.* (Repeat as often as needed.) |
| | If the student loses her/his place, point. (Repeat as often as needed.) |

# 14 DIBELS® Oral Reading Fluency
Level 1/Progress Monitoring 14 Retell

▶ *Now tell me as much as you can about the story you just read. Ready, begin.*

| | |
|---|---|
| *Timing* | 1-minute maximum. Start your stopwatch after telling the student to begin. Say **Stop** after 1 minute. |
| *Wait/ Reminder* | If the student stops or hesitates for 3 seconds, select *one* of the following (allowed one time):<br>—If the student has not said anything at all, provides a very limited response, or provides an off-track response, say **Tell me as much as you can about the story**.<br>—Otherwise, ask **Can you tell me anything more about the story?** |
| *Discontinue* | After the first reminder, if the student does not say anything or gets off track for 5 seconds, say **Thank you** and discontinue the task. |

## Dad's Surprise

▶ It was a great day for a sailboat ride. Meg put on her life vest and climbed into the boat. Dad pulled on a rope to lift the sail. The wind filled the cloth and pushed the boat away from the dock. Meg leaned over the side of the boat to feel the water. A wave splashed on her face. Meg laughed as she wiped the water out of her eyes.

Meg loved sailing with her dad. Each Saturday, they would sail to a spot on the other side of the lake. Dad would bring ham sandwiches for lunch. They would eat them as they sat on the sand. If it was a hot day, Meg and Dad went for a swim.

The boat had not gotten to the other side of the lake yet, but Dad let down the sail. The boat stopped. "I have a surprise for you," Dad said. He got out a fishing rod and tossed the line into the water. He gave the rod to Meg and she smiled. She had never been fishing. Soon, she felt a big tug.

"I caught something!" Meg yelled. She pulled a big fish onto the boat. Dad gave her a high five.

Then Dad raised the sail again and the boat began to glide across the water. Soon they arrived at the shore. Dad made a small fire to cook the fish. They had fish for lunch. It was a great picnic.

# 15 DIBELS® Oral Reading Fluency
Level 1/Progress Monitoring 15

Read the directions on page 83.

▶ **Begin testing. *Put your finger under the first word*** (point to the first word of the passage). ***Ready, begin.***

| | |
|---|---|
| *Timing* | 1 minute. Start your stopwatch after the student says the first word of the passage. Place a bracket ( ] ) and say ***Stop*** after 1 minute. |
| *Wait* | If no response in 3 seconds, say the word and mark it as incorrect. |
| *Discontinue* | If no words are read correctly in the first line, say ***Stop***, record a score of 0, and do not administer Retell. |
| | If fewer than 40 words are read correctly on any passage, use professional judgment whether to administer Retell for that passage. |
| *Reminders* | If the student stops (and it's not a hesitation on a specific item), say ***Keep going.*** (Repeat as often as needed.) |
| | If the student loses her/his place, point. (Repeat as often as needed.) |

# 15 DIBELS® Oral Reading Fluency
Level 1/Progress Monitoring 15 Retell

▶ *Now tell me as much as you can about the story you just read. Ready, begin.*

| | |
|---|---|
| **Timing** | 1-minute maximum. Start your stopwatch after telling the student to begin. Say **Stop** after 1 minute. |
| **Wait/ Reminder** | If the student stops or hesitates for 3 seconds, select *one* of the following (allowed one time):<br>—If the student has not said anything at all, provides a very limited response, or provides an off-track response, say **Tell me as much as you can about the story**.<br>—Otherwise, ask **Can you tell me anything more about the story?** |
| **Discontinue** | After the first reminder, if the student does not say anything or gets off track for 5 seconds, say **Thank you** and discontinue the task. |

## Kinds of Hats

▶ A hat sits on top of the head. There are many kinds of hats. Some hats have special jobs, and some hats are just for fun.

A hard hat keeps the head safe. It is made out of plastic. House builders wear this kind of hat. Things that fall cannot hurt their heads. Firefighters also use a hard hat. Their hats have a wide brim on the back to keep fire and heat away. You also wear a hard hat when you ride a bike. That hat is called a helmet.

Many workers wear hats that show the job they do. Some of these hats are made of cloth. Police officers wear a flat hat that is the same color as their uniform. Chefs wear tall white hats when they cook.

People use different hats to match the weather. Wool hats fit closely over the head. They keep the head and ears warm in the winter. Sun hats and baseball caps have a wide brim or bill. These hats shade the face and eyes from the sun in the summer.

Hats don't always have a job. Some are just for fun. Birthday party hats are made of paper. They have bright colors and cute pictures.

Next time you walk in the neighborhood, go on a hat hunt. You will be surprised at how many different hats you can find.

# 16 DIBELS® Oral Reading Fluency
Level 1/Progress Monitoring 16

Read the directions on page 83.

▶ Begin testing. *Put your finger under the first word* (point to the first word of the passage). *Ready, begin.*

| | |
|---|---|
| *Timing* | 1 minute. Start your stopwatch after the student says the first word of the passage. Place a bracket ( ] ) and say *Stop* after 1 minute. |
| *Wait* | If no response in 3 seconds, say the word and mark it as incorrect. |
| *Discontinue* | If no words are read correctly in the first line, say *Stop*, record a score of 0, and do not administer Retell. |
| | If fewer than 40 words are read correctly on any passage, use professional judgment whether to administer Retell for that passage. |
| *Reminders* | If the student stops (and it's not a hesitation on a specific item), say *Keep going.* (Repeat as often as needed.) |
| | If the student loses her/his place, point. (Repeat as often as needed.) |

# 16 DIBELS® Oral Reading Fluency
Level 1/Progress Monitoring 16 Retell

▶ *Now tell me as much as you can about the story you just read. Ready, begin.*

| | |
|---|---|
| **Timing** | 1-minute maximum. Start your stopwatch after telling the student to begin. Say **Stop** after 1 minute. |
| **Wait/ Reminder** | If the student stops or hesitates for 3 seconds, select *one* of the following (allowed one time):<br>—If the student has not said anything at all, provides a very limited response, or provides an off-track response, say **Tell me as much as you can about the story**.<br>—Otherwise, ask **Can you tell me anything more about the story?** |
| **Discontinue** | After the first reminder, if the student does not say anything or gets off track for 5 seconds, say **Thank you** and discontinue the task. |

# My Mom Is an Artist

▶ My mom makes things out of clay. She is an artist. Sometimes she has shows. In a show the clay objects she makes are put on display so many people can see them.

Clay comes in big blocks. My mom cuts off a lump of it. Then she folds it and rolls it to get it warm. Warm clay is easier to mold into shapes. Soon, the clay forms a soft ball.

Then Mom decides what to make. She can make lots of different things, but most often she will make a bowl. She places the clay ball on a wheel. The wheel goes round and round. Mom uses her hands to shape the clay into a bowl as the wheel spins.

When Mom is happy with the bowl, she lets it dry for several days. As the clay dries, it becomes hard. Next, Mom brushes a special paint on the bowl. The colors are light blue and mint green. Then Mom puts the bowl into a big oven that gets really hot. After the oven cools, Mom takes out the bowl. The paint colors are now bright blue and green.

Sometimes Mom lets me make things with clay. One time I made an elephant with big ears and a long trunk. I showed it to my teacher. She liked it a lot and put it on display in our class. Mom says this was my first show. She says I am an artist now, too.

# 17 DIBELS® Oral Reading Fluency
Level 1/Progress Monitoring 17

Read the directions on page 83.

▶ **Begin testing. *Put your finger under the first word*** (point to the first word of the passage)***. Ready, begin.***

| | |
|---|---|
| *Timing* | 1 minute. Start your stopwatch after the student says the first word of the passage. Place a bracket ( **]** ) and say ***Stop*** after 1 minute. |
| *Wait* | If no response in 3 seconds, say the word and mark it as incorrect. |
| *Discontinue* | If no words are read correctly in the first line, say ***Stop***, record a score of 0, and do not administer Retell. |
| | If fewer than 40 words are read correctly on any passage, use professional judgment whether to administer Retell for that passage. |
| *Reminders* | If the student stops (and it's not a hesitation on a specific item), say ***Keep going.*** (Repeat as often as needed.) |
| | If the student loses her/his place, point. (Repeat as often as needed.) |

# 17 DIBELS® Oral Reading Fluency
Level 1/Progress Monitoring 17 Retell

▶ *Now tell me as much as you can about the story you just read. Ready, begin.*

| | |
|---|---|
| **Timing** | 1-minute maximum. Start your stopwatch after telling the student to begin. Say **Stop** after 1 minute. |
| **Wait/ Reminder** | If the student stops or hesitates for 3 seconds, select *one* of the following (allowed one time):<br>—If the student has not said anything at all, provides a very limited response, or provides an off-track response, say **Tell me as much as you can about the story**.<br>—Otherwise, ask **Can you tell me anything more about the story?** |
| **Discontinue** | After the first reminder, if the student does not say anything or gets off track for 5 seconds, say **Thank you** and discontinue the task. |

# A Train Under the City

▶ The subway is a kind of train. It travels under the ground. The subway makes it fast and easy to get places in a big city.

It is easy to find the subway. In cities with a subway, there are lots of stops along the streets. The stops have big signs with stairs that take you down to the train tracks where the subway runs. To ride the subway you need a ticket. After you walk down the stairs you will see a ticket counter. There are also machines that sell tickets. The tickets are not expensive. When you have a ticket you can head toward the tracks and wait for the train.

When the train gets to your stop the doors will swoosh open. People will step off the train first. Now it is your turn to board the train. If there is a seat you can sit down. If not, you can stand. When the train gets to your stop, you get off and walk up the stairs back to the street.

The subway is very important. It helps people get around the city. It also means there is less traffic on the streets because people drive less. The subway is a great way to travel.

# 18 DIBELS® Oral Reading Fluency
Level 1/Progress Monitoring 18

Read the directions on page 83.

▶ **Begin testing. *Put your finger under the first word*** (point to the first word of the passage). ***Ready, begin.***

| | |
|---|---|
| *Timing* | 1 minute. Start your stopwatch after the student says the first word of the passage. Place a bracket ( ] ) and say ***Stop*** after 1 minute. |
| *Wait* | If no response in 3 seconds, say the word and mark it as incorrect. |
| *Discontinue* | If no words are read correctly in the first line, say ***Stop***, record a score of 0, and do not administer Retell. |
| | If fewer than 40 words are read correctly on any passage, use professional judgment whether to administer Retell for that passage. |
| *Reminders* | If the student stops (and it's not a hesitation on a specific item), say ***Keep going.*** (Repeat as often as needed.) |
| | If the student loses her/his place, point. (Repeat as often as needed.) |

# 18 DIBELS® Oral Reading Fluency
Level 1/Progress Monitoring 18 Retell

▶ *Now tell me as much as you can about the story you just read. Ready, begin.*

| | |
|---|---|
| **Timing** | 1-minute maximum. Start your stopwatch after telling the student to begin. Say **Stop** after 1 minute. |
| **Wait/ Reminder** | If the student stops or hesitates for 3 seconds, select *one* of the following (allowed one time):<br>—If the student has not said anything at all, provides a very limited response, or provides an off-track response, say **Tell me as much as you can about the story**.<br>—Otherwise, ask **Can you tell me anything more about the story?** |
| **Discontinue** | After the first reminder, if the student does not say anything or gets off track for 5 seconds, say **Thank you** and discontinue the task. |

# The School Bus

▶ Many children ride the bus to school every day. Without the school bus, it would be hard for some students to get to school at all. Other students may have difficulty getting to school on time. The bus gets students to school on time every day. The bus even picks children up near their house. After school, the bus takes them back home. It is easy to use the bus.

In addition to being easy to use, the school bus is also safe. In fact, school buses are one of the safest ways to travel. In most places, buses have warning lights. The lights tell other cars to stop when the bus is stopped. Boys and girls can then get off the bus and cross the road safely.

There is another reason to use the school bus. Riding the bus can be good for the Earth. Most large school buses can hold forty to sixty children. That's a lot more than a car. When children take the bus instead of going to school in a car, it uses less gas. It also makes less pollution.

It is easy to spot a school bus. They are painted bright yellow. If you see a school bus, think of the many good reasons to ride one.

# 19 DIBELS® Oral Reading Fluency
Level 1/Progress Monitoring 19

Read the directions on page 83.

▶ **Begin testing.** *Put your finger under the first word* (point to the first word of the passage). *Ready, begin.*

| | |
|---|---|
| *Timing* | 1 minute. Start your stopwatch after the student says the first word of the passage. Place a bracket ( **]** ) and say *Stop* after 1 minute. |
| *Wait* | If no response in 3 seconds, say the word and mark it as incorrect. |
| *Discontinue* | If no words are read correctly in the first line, say *Stop*, record a score of 0, and do not administer Retell. |
| | If fewer than 40 words are read correctly on any passage, use professional judgment whether to administer Retell for that passage. |
| *Reminders* | If the student stops (and it's not a hesitation on a specific item), say *Keep going.* (Repeat as often as needed.) |
| | If the student loses her/his place, point. (Repeat as often as needed.) |

# 19 DIBELS® Oral Reading Fluency
Level 1/Progress Monitoring 19 Retell

▶ *Now tell me as much as you can about the story you just read. Ready, begin.*

| | |
|---|---|
| *Timing* | 1-minute maximum. Start your stopwatch after telling the student to begin. Say **Stop** after 1 minute. |
| *Wait/ Reminder* | If the student stops or hesitates for 3 seconds, select *one* of the following (allowed one time):<br><br>—If the student has not said anything at all, provides a very limited response, or provides an off-track response, say **Tell me as much as you can about the story**.<br><br>—Otherwise, ask **Can you tell me anything more about the story?** |
| *Discontinue* | After the first reminder, if the student does not say anything or gets off track for 5 seconds, say **Thank you** and discontinue the task. |

## Star Pitcher

▶ My big sister is on the high school softball team. She is the pitcher. She tries to throw the ball so that the batter cannot hit it. My sister is a very good pitcher. In one game, she threw the ball so well that the other team could not get even one hit. After that game, she got her picture in the newspaper. The headline said "Star pitcher throws no-hitter." I liked that headline. It called my sister a star.

My parents and I go to as many of my sister's games as we can. We sit with all the other fans. Some of the fans go to my sister's school. Other fans just like to watch softball. All the fans clap when my sister throws the ball past the batter. If the batter misses the ball three times, she is out. When that happens, the fans cheer.

Being a star pitcher takes a lot of practice. Sometimes my sister takes me to practice with her. I sit very quietly and watch her work on her pitching. She also runs and works out to stay in shape. My sister says that being in shape is an important part of softball. She says it also keeps you healthy. Sometimes we go for short runs together so I can be in shape, too.

I like watching my sister play softball. Even when her team doesn't win, I know my sister is a star.

# 20 DIBELS® Oral Reading Fluency
Level 1/Progress Monitoring 20

Read the directions on page 83.

▶ **Begin testing.** *Put your finger under the first word* (point to the first word of the passage). *Ready, begin.*

| | |
|---|---|
| *Timing* | 1 minute. Start your stopwatch after the student says the first word of the passage. Place a bracket ( **]** ) and say *Stop* after 1 minute. |
| *Wait* | If no response in 3 seconds, say the word and mark it as incorrect. |
| *Discontinue* | If no words are read correctly in the first line, say *Stop*, record a score of 0, and do not administer Retell. |
| | If fewer than 40 words are read correctly on any passage, use professional judgment whether to administer Retell for that passage. |
| *Reminders* | If the student stops (and it's not a hesitation on a specific item), say *Keep going.* (Repeat as often as needed.) |
| | If the student loses her/his place, point. (Repeat as often as needed.) |

# 20 DIBELS® Oral Reading Fluency
Level 1/Progress Monitoring 20 Retell

▶ *Now tell me as much as you can about the story you just read. Ready, begin.*

| | |
|---|---|
| **Timing** | 1-minute maximum. Start your stopwatch after telling the student to begin. Say **Stop** after 1 minute. |
| **Wait/ Reminder** | If the student stops or hesitates for 3 seconds, select *one* of the following (allowed one time):<br>—If the student has not said anything at all, provides a very limited response, or provides an off-track response, say **Tell me as much as you can about the story**.<br>—Otherwise, ask **Can you tell me anything more about the story?** |
| **Discontinue** | After the first reminder, if the student does not say anything or gets off track for 5 seconds, say **Thank you** and discontinue the task. |

## DIBELS® Oral Reading Fluency
Level 2/Progress Monitoring

**Directions:** Make sure you have reviewed the scoring rules in the *DIBELS Next Assessment Manual* and have them available. Say these specific directions to the student:

▶ *I would like you to read a story to me. Please do your best reading. If you do not know a word, I will read the word for you. Keep reading until I say "stop." Be ready to tell me all about the story when you finish.*

▶ **Go to the next Progress Monitoring passage in the sequence.**

## Building Happy Places

▶ What do you do when you go to a playground? Maybe you run as quickly as you can to an empty swing, hop in, and soar to the sky. All children like to play and do fun things. There are lots of different ways to have fun. Matthew is a teenager who uses a wheelchair. He wanted some cool things for the playground that all children could use, so he did something about it.

When he was only six years old, Matthew had a great idea. He thought of a swing that all kids could use. It looks like a big boat. It can hold two kids in wheelchairs and six other children at the same time. He called it The Dreamer. The challenge for Matthew was to look at all the things on a playground and figure out how they could be made to work with a wheelchair. That way all children could play together.

Matthew gives his time to a group that builds playgrounds that are fun for all kids. The playgrounds have the usual swings that you would find in most places. They also have swings like The Dreamer. Instead of sandboxes on the ground, they have sand tables that children in wheelchairs can use. Matthew helps the group raise money so they can build more playgrounds. They built a special one called Friendship Place. It was built at Matthew's school.

# 1 DIBELS® Oral Reading Fluency
Level 2/Progress Monitoring 1

Read the directions on page 171.

▶ Begin testing. *Put your finger under the first word* (point to the first word of the passage). *Ready, begin.*

| | |
|---|---|
| **Timing** | 1 minute. Start your stopwatch after the student says the first word of the passage. Place a bracket ( **]** ) and say *Stop* after 1 minute. |
| **Wait** | If no response in 3 seconds, say the word and mark it as incorrect. |
| **Discontinue** | If no words are read correctly in the first line, say *Stop*, record a score of 0, and do not administer Retell. |
| | If fewer than 40 words are read correctly on any passage, use professional judgment whether to administer Retell for that passage. |
| **Reminders** | If the student stops (and it's not a hesitation on a specific item), say *Keep going.* (Repeat as often as needed.) |
| | If the student loses her/his place, point. (Repeat as often as needed.) |
| **Turn page** | If student reaches the end of the page (designated by triangles in the scoring booklet) before the minute is up, turn the page and continue on the next page. Otherwise, proceed to Retell when the minute is up. |

## Building Happy Places

For his work helping other children Matthew has been given many awards. He even had his picture on a cereal box. He feels proud that what he does helps all children play together and makes everyone happy.

---

# 1 DIBELS® Oral Reading Fluency
Level 2/Progress Monitoring 1 Retell

▶ *Now tell me as much as you can about the story you just read. Ready, begin.*

| | |
|---|---|
| *Timing* | 1-minute maximum. Start your stopwatch after telling the student to begin. Say **Stop** after 1 minute. |
| *Wait/ Reminder* | If the student stops or hesitates for 3 seconds, select *one* of the following (allowed one time):<br>—If the student has not said anything at all, provides a very limited response, or provides an off-track response, say **Tell me as much as you can about the story**.<br>—Otherwise, ask **Can you tell me anything more about the story?** |
| *Discontinue* | After the first reminder, if the student does not say anything or gets off track for 5 seconds, say **Thank you** and discontinue the task. |

## Luke Makes His Move

► After moving to a new neighborhood, Luke wanted to make some new friends. In his old neighborhood, all of his friends had played street hockey. Luke hoped to find someone to play street hockey.

Luke's stepdad had an idea. He said they should explore the neighborhood and see if they could find a game of street hockey. Luke thought it was a great idea. He and his stepdad went outside and walked around. After a short while, they turned the corner and found children playing hockey. It was just like his old home.

Luke stood on the side and watched the others play. He cheered for both teams whenever they made a goal or a difficult play. When one of the players had to go home, he asked Luke to play. Luke ran home to get his skates and stick.

Luke played goalie, his favorite position. He played his very best. He only let the other team score one goal. One time the other team was about to score and there was no one but him to defend the goal. The other team came toward Luke, faster and faster. He watched carefully to see where they were going to go. He leaped at the last second and stopped them from scoring. His whole team cheered.

After the game, they all went down to the corner store and got a

**2** **DIBELS® Oral Reading Fluency**
Level 2/Progress Monitoring 2

Read the directions on page 171.

▶ Begin testing. *Put your finger under the first word* (point to the first word of the passage). *Ready, begin.*

| | |
|---|---|
| *Timing* | 1 minute. Start your stopwatch after the student says the first word of the passage. Place a bracket ( **]** ) and say *Stop* after 1 minute. |
| *Wait* | If no response in 3 seconds, say the word and mark it as incorrect. |
| *Discontinue* | If no words are read correctly in the first line, say *Stop*, record a score of 0, and do not administer Retell.<br><br>If fewer than 40 words are read correctly on any passage, use professional judgment whether to administer Retell for that passage. |
| *Reminders* | If the student stops (and it's not a hesitation on a specific item), say *Keep going.* (Repeat as often as needed.)<br><br>If the student loses her/his place, point. (Repeat as often as needed.) |
| *Turn page* | If student reaches the end of the page (designated by triangles in the scoring booklet) before the minute is up, turn the page and continue on the next page. Otherwise, proceed to Retell when the minute is up. |

DORF/Level 2

# Luke Makes His Move

snack. Everyone talked about the game. They decided to play again the next day. Luke was glad he had made new friends.

DORF/Level 2

# 2 DIBELS® Oral Reading Fluency
Level 2/Progress Monitoring 2 Retell

▶ *Now tell me as much as you can about the story you just read. Ready, begin.*

| | |
|---|---|
| *Timing* | 1-minute maximum. Start your stopwatch after telling the student to begin. Say **Stop** after 1 minute. |
| *Wait/ Reminder* | If the student stops or hesitates for 3 seconds, select *one* of the following (allowed one time):<br>—If the student has not said anything at all, provides a very limited response, or provides an off-track response, say **Tell me as much as you can about the story**.<br>—Otherwise, ask **Can you tell me anything more about the story?** |
| *Discontinue* | After the first reminder, if the student does not say anything or gets off track for 5 seconds, say **Thank you** and discontinue the task. |

## My Pen Pal

▶ I have a pen pal who lives in a faraway place. He lives all the way across the ocean in a different country. He tells me about what it is like to live in his country. I tell him about what it is like to live in mine. I live in India. In many ways, our lives are very similar. We both go to school and both enjoy listening to music. There are also ways in which our lives are different.

My pen pal and I usually write to each other at least once a month, but I waited longer to write him a letter this month. I was waiting for my loose tooth to fall out. I wiggled my tooth a lot. It didn't want to come out. I tried different tricks, but they did not work. At last, while I was eating something sticky, the tooth came out.

Then I tossed my tooth up on the roof. I asked a sparrow to take the tooth and give me a new one. This was a custom in my country. When a new tooth began to grow I thanked the sparrow.

I wrote a long letter to my pen pal about losing my tooth. He wrote back and told me about his tradition when he loses a tooth. He said he puts the tooth under his pillow. During the night someone takes the tooth away. What a strange custom! I like learning about different countries.

# 3 DIBELS® Oral Reading Fluency
Level 2/Progress Monitoring 3

Read the directions on page 171.

▶ **Begin testing. *Put your finger under the first word*** (point to the first word of the passage). ***Ready, begin.***

| | |
|---|---|
| *Timing* | 1 minute. Start your stopwatch after the student says the first word of the passage. Place a bracket ( **]** ) and say ***Stop*** after 1 minute. |
| *Wait* | If no response in 3 seconds, say the word and mark it as incorrect. |
| *Discontinue* | If no words are read correctly in the first line, say ***Stop***, record a score of 0, and do not administer Retell. |
| | If fewer than 40 words are read correctly on any passage, use professional judgment whether to administer Retell for that passage. |
| *Reminders* | If the student stops (and it's not a hesitation on a specific item), say ***Keep going.*** (Repeat as often as needed.) |
| | If the student loses her/his place, point. (Repeat as often as needed.) |

# 3 DIBELS® Oral Reading Fluency
Level 2/Progress Monitoring 3 Retell

▶ *Now tell me as much as you can about the story you just read. Ready, begin.*

| | |
|---|---|
| *Timing* | 1-minute maximum. Start your stopwatch after telling the student to begin. Say **Stop** after 1 minute. |
| *Wait/ Reminder* | If the student stops or hesitates for 3 seconds, select *one* of the following (allowed one time):<br><br>—If the student has not said anything at all, provides a very limited response, or provides an off-track response, say **Tell me as much as you can about the story**.<br><br>—Otherwise, ask **Can you tell me anything more about the story?** |
| *Discontinue* | After the first reminder, if the student does not say anything or gets off track for 5 seconds, say **Thank you** and discontinue the task. |

# Life on the River

▶ I live by a big river. The river is very important to my family. My name is Ling, and I live in a village in Asia. There are thirty houses in my village. We use the water to wash ourselves and our clothes. We also use the water for our plants since a lot of our food comes from crops we grow. The river gives us water for drinking, too. Our boats travel up and down the river, taking us from village to village. We also play in the river!

You may wonder what life is like for me. I wake up to a rooster instead of an alarm clock. Our rooster wakes us at four in the morning, and we immediately get busy. I help prepare breakfast for the rest of the family. After we eat, we feed the animals. Sometimes there is corn to grind. When I finish these chores, I go into the field to help where I can. The younger kids stay home with our grandparents.

In our village, children are expected to help the family. There is always work to do. On days when I am not helping in the field, I babysit or clean the house. In the evening, I help gather firewood to cook our dinner. After dinner, we sit with our grandparents. They tell us stories about how things came to be. My favorite story is how the river got its color. I hope one day I can share the story with you.

# 4 DIBELS® Oral Reading Fluency
Level 2/Progress Monitoring 4

Read the directions on page 171.

▶ **Begin testing. *Put your finger under the first word*** (point to the first word of the passage). ***Ready, begin.***

| | |
|---|---|
| *Timing* | 1 minute. Start your stopwatch after the student says the first word of the passage. Place a bracket ( ] ) and say ***Stop*** after 1 minute. |
| *Wait* | If no response in 3 seconds, say the word and mark it as incorrect. |
| *Discontinue* | If no words are read correctly in the first line, say ***Stop***, record a score of 0, and do not administer Retell.<br><br>If fewer than 40 words are read correctly on any passage, use professional judgment whether to administer Retell for that passage. |
| *Reminders* | If the student stops (and it's not a hesitation on a specific item), say ***Keep going.*** (Repeat as often as needed.)<br><br>If the student loses her/his place, point. (Repeat as often as needed.) |

DORF/Level 2

# 4 DIBELS® Oral Reading Fluency
Level 2/Progress Monitoring 4 Retell

▶ *Now tell me as much as you can about the story you just read. Ready, begin.*

| | |
|---|---|
| *Timing* | 1-minute maximum. Start your stopwatch after telling the student to begin. Say **Stop** after 1 minute. |
| *Wait/ Reminder* | If the student stops or hesitates for 3 seconds, select *one* of the following (allowed one time):<br>—If the student has not said anything at all, provides a very limited response, or provides an off-track response, say **Tell me as much as you can about the story**.<br>—Otherwise, ask **Can you tell me anything more about the story?** |
| *Discontinue* | After the first reminder, if the student does not say anything or gets off track for 5 seconds, say **Thank you** and discontinue the task. |

DORF/Level 2

# A Day for Trees

▶ Picture yourself walking through the woods. Rays of sun stream in through the trees, but mostly it is shady. You welcome the coolness of the shade. The leaves crunch under your feet, and animals scurry about.

Now think about what this scene would be like without any trees. Is it hard to imagine? Trees are very important. They give us shade. Trees are home to many animals. Trees help keep our air clean, too.

Trees are so important that they have their own special day. It is called Arbor Day. On this day, people plant trees. Some people choose to plant a tiny seed in the soil. They give the seed water and watch it grow. Other people choose to plant a small tree that has already started to grow. They dig a small hole and carefully put the roots into the soil. They cover up the roots and give the tree water.

You may wonder when Arbor Day happens. That depends on where you live. Many states have this special day in the spring. That is the best time to plant trees in those states. Some states have better times for planting trees. If you live where the weather is always warm, your special tree day may be in the fall or even in the winter. No matter when your state has its special tree day, make sure you plant a tree.

# 5 DIBELS® Oral Reading Fluency
Level 2/Progress Monitoring 5

Read the directions on page 171.

▶ **Begin testing.** *Put your finger under the first word* (point to the first word of the passage). *Ready, begin.*

| | |
|---|---|
| *Timing* | 1 minute. Start your stopwatch after the student says the first word of the passage. Place a bracket ( **]** ) and say *Stop* after 1 minute. |
| *Wait* | If no response in 3 seconds, say the word and mark it as incorrect. |
| *Discontinue* | If no words are read correctly in the first line, say *Stop*, record a score of 0, and do not administer Retell. |
| | If fewer than 40 words are read correctly on any passage, use professional judgment whether to administer Retell for that passage. |
| *Reminders* | If the student stops (and it's not a hesitation on a specific item), say *Keep going.* (Repeat as often as needed.) |
| | If the student loses her/his place, point. (Repeat as often as needed.) |

DORF/Level 2

# 5 DIBELS® Oral Reading Fluency
Level 2/Progress Monitoring 5 Retell

▶ *Now tell me as much as you can about the story you just read. Ready, begin.*

| | |
|---|---|
| **Timing** | 1-minute maximum. Start your stopwatch after telling the student to begin. Say **Stop** after 1 minute. |
| **Wait/ Reminder** | If the student stops or hesitates for 3 seconds, select *one* of the following (allowed one time):<br>—If the student has not said anything at all, provides a very limited response, or provides an off-track response, say **Tell me as much as you can about the story**.<br>—Otherwise, ask **Can you tell me anything more about the story?** |
| **Discontinue** | After the first reminder, if the student does not say anything or gets off track for 5 seconds, say **Thank you** and discontinue the task. |

DORF/Level 2

# Making Orange Juice

▶ What is the best part about eating an orange? There are many things to choose from. Your eye may notice the fruit's bright orange skin. Just the sight of an orange may be enough to make your mouth water! When you peel off the rough skin, the sweet smell tickles your nose. When you bite into the fruit, the juice wakes up your taste buds.

There is another way to enjoy the taste of an orange. You can make orange juice. Making orange juice is easy and fun, and you only need a few things. You need six oranges, and an adult to help cut them. You will also need a pitcher and some cups.

First, squeeze the oranges to get them soft. Then wash the oranges. Have the adult help you cut the oranges in half safely. Take out the seeds from each half. Now you are ready to squeeze out the juice. Grip half an orange and squeeze the juice into a pitcher. Turn the orange and squeeze again. Keep squeezing until no more juice comes out. Repeat with each orange half.

You have some choices when you make orange juice. If you like, you can scrape the orange with a spoon and add the fruit to the juice. Or if you do not like pulp, place a strainer over the pitcher. This will catch all the orange bits, and only juice will fall into the pitcher. If you

# 6 DIBELS® Oral Reading Fluency
Level 2/Progress Monitoring 6

Read the directions on page 171.

▶ **Begin testing.** *Put your finger under the first word* (point to the first word of the passage). *Ready, begin.*

| | |
|---|---|
| *Timing* | 1 minute. Start your stopwatch after the student says the first word of the passage. Place a bracket ( ] ) and say *Stop* after 1 minute. |
| *Wait* | If no response in 3 seconds, say the word and mark it as incorrect. |
| *Discontinue* | If no words are read correctly in the first line, say *Stop*, record a score of 0, and do not administer Retell. |
| | If fewer than 40 words are read correctly on any passage, use professional judgment whether to administer Retell for that passage. |
| *Reminders* | If the student stops (and it's not a hesitation on a specific item), say *Keep going.* (Repeat as often as needed.) |
| | If the student loses her/his place, point. (Repeat as often as needed.) |
| *Turn page* | If student reaches the end of the page (designated by triangles in the scoring booklet) before the minute is up, turn the page and continue on the next page. Otherwise, proceed to Retell when the minute is up. |

DORF/Level 2

## Making Orange Juice

want cold orange juice, add ice to the pitcher.

Now you are ready to pour the orange juice into a cup. You may want to share with a friend. Drink the juice and enjoy!

_____

DORF/Level 2

# 6 DIBELS® Oral Reading Fluency
Level 2/Progress Monitoring 6 Retell

▶ *Now tell me as much as you can about the story you just read. Ready, begin.*

| | |
|---|---|
| *Timing* | 1-minute maximum. Start your stopwatch after telling the student to begin. Say **Stop** after 1 minute. |
| *Wait/ Reminder* | If the student stops or hesitates for 3 seconds, select *one* of the following (allowed one time):<br>—If the student has not said anything at all, provides a very limited response, or provides an off-track response, say **Tell me as much as you can about the story**.<br>—Otherwise, ask **Can you tell me anything more about the story?** |
| *Discontinue* | After the first reminder, if the student does not say anything or gets off track for 5 seconds, say **Thank you** and discontinue the task. |

# Kim Gets Ready

▶ What is your house like in the morning? In my family, the morning is a busy time. We children get ready for school while my dad and uncle get ready for their jobs. They are fishermen. My name is Kim, and I live in a country called Vietnam.

In the morning, my family eats breakfast together. We do not use plates or forks. Instead, our table is set with deep bowls and chopsticks. For breakfast, we may eat soup or rice with meat or fish. We often have fruit, too.

After breakfast, we put on our school uniforms. Then my sister and I ride our bikes to our school. My older sister and brother walk to their school. Because they are older, they go to a different school.

Where I live, children go to school six days a week. We do not go to school on Sundays. In my classroom, I sit with one other child at a desk. There are 30 children in my class. We have lessons in math and language. We also learn about science and history. Each day, we take a break from our lessons and do gymnastics. School teaches us to be active.

Students in my school also learn to be responsible. We take turns cleaning. When it is my turn, I get to school early. I may sweep the floor or empty the trashcans.

# 7 DIBELS® Oral Reading Fluency
Level 2/Progress Monitoring 7

Read the directions on page 171.

▶ **Begin testing. *Put your finger under the first word*** (point to the first word of the passage). ***Ready, begin.***

| | |
|---|---|
| *Timing* | 1 minute. Start your stopwatch after the student says the first word of the passage. Place a bracket ( **]** ) and say ***Stop*** after 1 minute. |
| *Wait* | If no response in 3 seconds, say the word and mark it as incorrect. |
| *Discontinue* | If no words are read correctly in the first line, say ***Stop***, record a score of 0, and do not administer Retell. |
| | If fewer than 40 words are read correctly on any passage, use professional judgment whether to administer Retell for that passage. |
| *Reminders* | If the student stops (and it's not a hesitation on a specific item), say ***Keep going.*** (Repeat as often as needed.) |
| | If the student loses her/his place, point. (Repeat as often as needed.) |

# 7 DIBELS® Oral Reading Fluency
Level 2/Progress Monitoring 7 Retell

▶ *Now tell me as much as you can about the story you just read. Ready, begin.*

| | |
|---|---|
| **Timing** | 1-minute maximum. Start your stopwatch after telling the student to begin. Say **Stop** after 1 minute. |
| **Wait/ Reminder** | If the student stops or hesitates for 3 seconds, select *one* of the following (allowed one time):<br>—If the student has not said anything at all, provides a very limited response, or provides an off-track response, say **Tell me as much as you can about the story**.<br>—Otherwise, ask **Can you tell me anything more about the story?** |
| **Discontinue** | After the first reminder, if the student does not say anything or gets off track for 5 seconds, say **Thank you** and discontinue the task. |

DORF/Level 2

# Dear Diary

▶ Dear Diary,

Today is Monday. We're playing basketball in gym class tomorrow. It is sure to be the worst day of my life! Today we learned the game's rules, and tomorrow we play. I'm hoping I won't have to play. Maybe I will get sick. I did cough earlier today.

I tried to tell the teacher that I'm good at tap dancing, not basketball, but she wouldn't listen. She told me to try my best.

Dear Diary,

Today is Tuesday. Believe it or not, today was one of my better days. When I woke this morning, I asked Dad to take me to the dentist, the doctor, or anyone as long as it was during PE class. Dad would not agree, and instead, he gave me basketball tips. I tried to listen, but the sound of my pounding heart filled my head.

All day I suffered, waiting for gym class. Each minute felt like an hour. Finally, we lined up and walked to the gym.

Soon I was holding a basketball, bouncing it up and down. When we took our practice shots, the teacher showed me how to shoot the ball. The first time I tried, the ball went in the basket! I started to believe that

# 8 DIBELS® Oral Reading Fluency
Level 2/Progress Monitoring 8

Read the directions on page 171.

▶ **Begin testing.** *Put your finger under the first word* (point to the first word of the passage). *Ready, begin.*

| | |
|---|---|
| *Timing* | 1 minute. Start your stopwatch after the student says the first word of the passage. Place a bracket ( ] ) and say *Stop* after 1 minute. |
| *Wait* | If no response in 3 seconds, say the word and mark it as incorrect. |
| *Discontinue* | If no words are read correctly in the first line, say *Stop*, record a score of 0, and do not administer Retell. |
| | If fewer than 40 words are read correctly on any passage, use professional judgment whether to administer Retell for that passage. |
| *Reminders* | If the student stops (and it's not a hesitation on a specific item), say *Keep going.* (Repeat as often as needed.) |
| | If the student loses her/his place, point. (Repeat as often as needed.) |
| *Turn page* | If student reaches the end of the page (designated by triangles in the scoring booklet) before the minute is up, turn the page and continue on the next page. Otherwise, proceed to Retell when the minute is up. |

## Dear Diary

maybe I could play basketball.

    Once the game started, time passed quickly. I was surprised when I heard the long whistle meaning that the game was over. When I shook hands with the players, some of them said, "Good game!" The teacher looked at me and winked. You never know how you feel about something new until you try!

---

DORF/Level 2

# 8 DIBELS® Oral Reading Fluency
Level 2/Progress Monitoring 8 Retell

▶ *Now tell me as much as you can about the story you just read. Ready, begin.*

| | |
|---|---|
| **Timing** | 1-minute maximum. Start your stopwatch after telling the student to begin. Say **Stop** after 1 minute. |
| **Wait/ Reminder** | If the student stops or hesitates for 3 seconds, select *one* of the following (allowed one time):<br>—If the student has not said anything at all, provides a very limited response, or provides an off-track response, say **Tell me as much as you can about the story**.<br>—Otherwise, ask **Can you tell me anything more about the story?** |
| **Discontinue** | After the first reminder, if the student does not say anything or gets off track for 5 seconds, say **Thank you** and discontinue the task. |

# Circus Tickets

▶ The sign said, "Get a free ticket to the circus." Jake showed the sign to his brother, Adam. The library wanted to encourage children to keep reading in the summer. Any student who read five books would be given a free ticket to the circus. The boys had never been to the circus. It was something they had always wanted to do. They showed the sign to their mother. She agreed to take them to the library to get books to read.

The brothers went to their local library for the first time. With help from their mother, they got library cards. Then they began looking for books. Jake did not know what to read. He searched the shelves and found a biography about a swimmer. Jake loved to swim. He glanced through the book and thought it was something he would enjoy reading. Adam was not sure what to read either, but he found a mystery that he thought would be good to read.

Back at home, the boys sat on the couch and started reading. It was quiet in the room. They thought they would be bored without TV, but they were wrong. They read for an hour until their mother called them to dinner.

Jake and Adam quickly finished their books. They went back to the library for more. In two weeks, they had read five books and

# 9 DIBELS® Oral Reading Fluency
Level 2/Progress Monitoring 9

Read the directions on page 171.

▶ **Begin testing. *Put your finger under the first word*** (point to the first word of the passage). ***Ready, begin.***

| | |
|---|---|
| *Timing* | 1 minute. Start your stopwatch after the student says the first word of the passage. Place a bracket ( **]** ) and say ***Stop*** after 1 minute. |
| *Wait* | If no response in 3 seconds, say the word and mark it as incorrect. |
| *Discontinue* | If no words are read correctly in the first line, say ***Stop***, record a score of 0, and do not administer Retell. |
| | If fewer than 40 words are read correctly on any passage, use professional judgment whether to administer Retell for that passage. |
| *Reminders* | If the student stops (and it's not a hesitation on a specific item), say ***Keep going.*** (Repeat as often as needed.) |
| | If the student loses her/his place, point. (Repeat as often as needed.) |
| *Turn page* | If student reaches the end of the page (designated by triangles in the scoring booklet) before the minute is up, turn the page and continue on the next page. Otherwise, proceed to Retell when the minute is up. |

## Circus Tickets

earned their circus tickets. When the circus came to town, they proudly presented their tickets at the ticket booth. On the way in, a clown gave them a high five. It was going to be a great show!

---

DORF/Level 2

# 9 DIBELS® Oral Reading Fluency
Level 2/Progress Monitoring 9 Retell

▶ *Now tell me as much as you can about the story you just read. Ready, begin.*

| | |
|---|---|
| *Timing* | 1-minute maximum. Start your stopwatch after telling the student to begin. Say **Stop** after 1 minute. |
| *Wait/ Reminder* | If the student stops or hesitates for 3 seconds, select *one* of the following (allowed one time):<br>—If the student has not said anything at all, provides a very limited response, or provides an off-track response, say **Tell me as much as you can about the story**.<br>—Otherwise, ask **Can you tell me anything more about the story?** |
| *Discontinue* | After the first reminder, if the student does not say anything or gets off track for 5 seconds, say **Thank you** and discontinue the task. |

# Bats Are Not Birds

▶ What has wings and can fly? If you said a bird, you are correct, but another correct answer is a bat. Bats and birds are both animals that have wings and can fly. While they have some things in common, they are also different in many ways.

Birds have feathers and lay eggs in a nest. The baby birds hatch from the eggs. Bats do not have feathers and do not lay eggs. They are mammals. Like other mammals, bats have fur on their bodies. The baby bats drink milk from their mothers. They do not live in a nest, but in caves and trees.

If you were to look at the bones of a bat and a bird, you would notice differences. A bat's bones look like the bones in your own arm and hand. The bones look like long fingers. Instead of feathers, a thin skin covers the bones. A bird's bones are shorter. They are covered and supported by feathers.

You can see another difference between bats and birds when you look at their mouths. Most bats have teeth to chew insects or fruit. Birds have bills. Their bills have different shapes depending on what they eat.

A final difference is when you see the animal flying. Do you see something flying at night? It may be a bat. They fly at night using echoes

# 10 DIBELS® Oral Reading Fluency
Level 2/Progress Monitoring 10

Read the directions on page 171.

▶ **Begin testing.** *Put your finger under the first word* (point to the first word of the passage). *Ready, begin.*

| | |
|---|---|
| *Timing* | 1 minute. Start your stopwatch after the student says the first word of the passage. Place a bracket ( **]** ) and say *Stop* after 1 minute. |
| *Wait* | If no response in 3 seconds, say the word and mark it as incorrect. |
| *Discontinue* | If no words are read correctly in the first line, say *Stop*, record a score of 0, and do not administer Retell. |
| | If fewer than 40 words are read correctly on any passage, use professional judgment whether to administer Retell for that passage. |
| *Reminders* | If the student stops (and it's not a hesitation on a specific item), say *Keep going.* (Repeat as often as needed.) |
| | If the student loses her/his place, point. (Repeat as often as needed.) |
| *Turn page* | If student reaches the end of the page (designated by triangles in the scoring booklet) before the minute is up, turn the page and continue on the next page. Otherwise, proceed to Retell when the minute is up. |

## Bats Are Not Birds

instead of sight. Birds usually fly during the day. Some have a very keen sense of sight.

The next time you see something flying, ask yourself, "Is this a bat or a bird?" Remember, they are not the same!

DORF/Level 2

# 10 DIBELS® Oral Reading Fluency
Level 2/Progress Monitoring 10 Retell

▶ *Now tell me as much as you can about the story you just read. Ready, begin.*

| | |
|---|---|
| *Timing* | 1-minute maximum. Start your stopwatch after telling the student to begin. Say **Stop** after 1 minute. |
| *Wait/ Reminder* | If the student stops or hesitates for 3 seconds, select *one* of the following (allowed one time): <br>—If the student has not said anything at all, provides a very limited response, or provides an off-track response, say **Tell me as much as you can about the story**. <br>—Otherwise, ask **Can you tell me anything more about the story?** |
| *Discontinue* | After the first reminder, if the student does not say anything or gets off track for 5 seconds, say **Thank you** and discontinue the task. |

# Cooking School

▶ Cheese and crackers make a great snack, but not if you eat them every day. When Jake came home from school, he ate cheese and crackers. One day, he told his grandmother Nana he was tired of the same snack. He asked her to teach him how to make a different snack. When a smile spread across Nana's face, Jake wondered what she was thinking.

Nana told Jake to wash his hands. Then she told him to get peanut butter while she got non-fat dry milk and honey. They mixed the three foods together. Then Nana told Jake something surprising. She told him to play with his food! Jake molded the dough into a dinosaur and then into a flower. Then he ate the dough! "That was fun!" Jake said.

The next day, Jake told his friends about Nana's cooking lesson. They all wanted to have a lesson from Nana, too. Jake talked to Nana about his friends' requests, and they decided to have a cooking school.

Jake and his friends gathered in the kitchen on Saturday. Nana had an apron for each child. She had four stations set up. At each station, the kids learned how to make a healthy and delicious snack. The children had so much fun, they asked Nana to have cooking school once a month. Nana was happy to agree. No more cheese and crackers for Jake!

# 11 DIBELS® Oral Reading Fluency
Level 2/Progress Monitoring 11

Read the directions on page 171.

▶ **Begin testing.** *Put your finger under the first word* (point to the first word of the passage). *Ready, begin.*

| | |
|---|---|
| *Timing* | 1 minute. Start your stopwatch after the student says the first word of the passage. Place a bracket ( **]** ) and say *Stop* after 1 minute. |
| *Wait* | If no response in 3 seconds, say the word and mark it as incorrect. |
| *Discontinue* | If no words are read correctly in the first line, say *Stop*, record a score of 0, and do not administer Retell. |
| | If fewer than 40 words are read correctly on any passage, use professional judgment whether to administer Retell for that passage. |
| *Reminders* | If the student stops (and it's not a hesitation on a specific item), say *Keep going.* (Repeat as often as needed.) |
| | If the student loses her/his place, point. (Repeat as often as needed.) |

# 11 DIBELS® Oral Reading Fluency
Level 2/Progress Monitoring 11 Retell

▶ *Now tell me as much as you can about the story you just read. Ready, begin.*

| | |
|---|---|
| *Timing* | 1-minute maximum. Start your stopwatch after telling the student to begin. Say ***Stop*** after 1 minute. |
| *Wait/ Reminder* | If the student stops or hesitates for 3 seconds, select *one* of the following (allowed one time): <br>—If the student has not said anything at all, provides a very limited response, or provides an off-track response, say ***Tell me as much as you can about the story***. <br>—Otherwise, ask ***Can you tell me anything more about the story?*** |
| *Discontinue* | After the first reminder, if the student does not say anything or gets off track for 5 seconds, say ***Thank you*** and discontinue the task. |

# Writing Your Own Book

▶ Children enjoy reading books, but very few have written one. It is not hard to do. All you need is some paper and colored pencils or markers and a good idea. You can create your own book.

You may already have a great idea for your book. If not, you can write a book that tells something about yourself. You can write how old you are, what color your hair and eyes are, and how tall you are. You can paste a picture of yourself to the page. If you don't have a picture, draw one. Next, write about your school. Write down your grade, teacher's name, and what you are learning. Draw a picture of your teacher or of your favorite school subject. On the next page, you can write about your friends. Or, you can write about things you like to do at home. You can also write about your favorite food, movie, or book.

These are just some ideas of what to include in your book. There are many more things you can write about. Think about a story you would like to tell. Tell about things that interest you. You might get other ideas from looking in books. When you are done with your book, staple the pages together. You could also punch holes in the pages and tie them together with yarn. As you can see, making a book is fun and easy.

# 12 DIBELS® Oral Reading Fluency
Level 2/Progress Monitoring 12

Read the directions on page 171.

▶ **Begin testing.** *Put your finger under the first word* (point to the first word of the passage). *Ready, begin.*

| | |
|---|---|
| *Timing* | 1 minute. Start your stopwatch after the student says the first word of the passage. Place a bracket ( **]** ) and say *Stop* after 1 minute. |
| *Wait* | If no response in 3 seconds, say the word and mark it as incorrect. |
| *Discontinue* | If no words are read correctly in the first line, say *Stop*, record a score of 0, and do not administer Retell.<br><br>If fewer than 40 words are read correctly on any passage, use professional judgment whether to administer Retell for that passage. |
| *Reminders* | If the student stops (and it's not a hesitation on a specific item), say *Keep going.* (Repeat as often as needed.)<br>If the student loses her/his place, point. (Repeat as often as needed.) |

DORF/Level 2

# 12 DIBELS® Oral Reading Fluency
Level 2/Progress Monitoring 12 Retell

▶ *Now tell me as much as you can about the story you just read. Ready, begin.*

| | |
|---|---|
| *Timing* | 1-minute maximum. Start your stopwatch after telling the student to begin. Say **Stop** after 1 minute. |
| *Wait/ Reminder* | If the student stops or hesitates for 3 seconds, select *one* of the following (allowed one time):<br><br>—If the student has not said anything at all, provides a very limited response, or provides an off-track response, say **Tell me as much as you can about the story**.<br><br>—Otherwise, ask **Can you tell me anything more about the story?** |
| *Discontinue* | After the first reminder, if the student does not say anything or gets off track for 5 seconds, say **Thank you** and discontinue the task. |

# In Space for an Hour

► I went to a movie where I felt like I was really in space. I had always wondered what it would feel like to travel in a rocket. After my experience, I can imagine it even better.

We were on vacation visiting my mother's sister in a big city. We don't get to go to the city very often, so my aunt said she would take us to all the special things that we don't have at home. I was surprised when my aunt said we were going to a movie. I told her that we had movies at home. My aunt just smiled. She said this was a special type of movie.

The theater looked like any other until we went inside. The screen was enormous. It had to be the biggest screen I'd ever seen. It went from the floor to the ceiling, and it curved. I stared in astonishment. "What is this going to be like?" I wondered.

Then the lights went out. Suddenly we felt like we were inside a space shuttle. We heard the countdown. We heard the roar of the rockets. When they called, "Blast off!" it felt like we had really blasted off. It looked and sounded so real. For one hour I felt I was on a space mission. We went all the way to the moon and back. It was a trip I'll always remember.

# 13 DIBELS® Oral Reading Fluency
Level 2/Progress Monitoring 13

Read the directions on page 171.

▶ Begin testing. *Put your finger under the first word* (point to the first word of the passage). *Ready, begin.*

| | |
|---|---|
| *Timing* | 1 minute. Start your stopwatch after the student says the first word of the passage. Place a bracket ( ] ) and say *Stop* after 1 minute. |
| *Wait* | If no response in 3 seconds, say the word and mark it as incorrect. |
| *Discontinue* | If no words are read correctly in the first line, say *Stop*, record a score of 0, and do not administer Retell. |
| | If fewer than 40 words are read correctly on any passage, use professional judgment whether to administer Retell for that passage. |
| *Reminders* | If the student stops (and it's not a hesitation on a specific item), say *Keep going.* (Repeat as often as needed.) |
| | If the student loses her/his place, point. (Repeat as often as needed.) |

# 13 DIBELS® Oral Reading Fluency
Level 2/Progress Monitoring 13 Retell

▶ *Now tell me as much as you can about the story you just read. Ready, begin.*

| Timing | 1-minute maximum. Start your stopwatch after telling the student to begin. Say **Stop** after 1 minute. |
|---|---|
| Wait/ Reminder | If the student stops or hesitates for 3 seconds, select *one* of the following (allowed one time):<br>—If the student has not said anything at all, provides a very limited response, or provides an off-track response, say **Tell me as much as you can about the story**.<br>—Otherwise, ask **Can you tell me anything more about the story?** |
| Discontinue | After the first reminder, if the student does not say anything or gets off track for 5 seconds, say **Thank you** and discontinue the task. |

DORF/Level 2

# Wind Power

▶ The wind is a source of power. It helps kites to fly, and boats to sail. In some places, wind power is used to make electricity. People are working to find ways to help us get more power from the wind.

There are many reasons why turning wind into power can be a good idea. We will never run out of wind. It will always blow. Most other ways to make power use resources that could run out. Coal and natural gas are two common examples. One day we might run out of them. We can count on the wind because it will always blow.

Windmills are what help us turn wind into electricity. When the wind blows, it turns the blades on the mill. This spinning makes a small amount of electricity. When you put a lot of windmills together, you can make enough power for a lot of people.

A wind farm is a place with a lot of windmills. You can find wind farms in places that are very windy. The windmills are very tall, and their blades are very long. Some have blades that are as long as a football field.

There are a few problems with wind power. Some days there is not much wind, and you may flip a light switch and have no light. Also, wind power costs more than other kinds of power. People are working to fix

# 14 DIBELS® Oral Reading Fluency
Level 2/Progress Monitoring 14

Read the directions on page 171.

▶ **Begin testing.** *Put your finger under the first word* (point to the first word of the passage). *Ready, begin.*

| | |
|---|---|
| *Timing* | 1 minute. Start your stopwatch after the student says the first word of the passage. Place a bracket ( **]** ) and say *Stop* after 1 minute. |
| *Wait* | If no response in 3 seconds, say the word and mark it as incorrect. |
| *Discontinue* | If no words are read correctly in the first line, say *Stop*, record a score of 0, and do not administer Retell. |
| | If fewer than 40 words are read correctly on any passage, use professional judgment whether to administer Retell for that passage. |
| *Reminders* | If the student stops (and it's not a hesitation on a specific item), say *Keep going.* (Repeat as often as needed.) |
| | If the student loses her/his place, point. (Repeat as often as needed.) |
| *Turn page* | If student reaches the end of the page (designated by triangles in the scoring booklet) before the minute is up, turn the page and continue on the next page. Otherwise, proceed to Retell when the minute is up. |

## Wind Power

these problems. One day, when you turn on your bedroom light, your lamp may light up due to power from the wind.

DORF/Level 2

# 14 DIBELS® Oral Reading Fluency
Level 2/Progress Monitoring 14 Retell

▶ *Now tell me as much as you can about the story you just read. Ready, begin.*

| | |
|---|---|
| **Timing** | 1-minute maximum. Start your stopwatch after telling the student to begin. Say **Stop** after 1 minute. |
| **Wait/ Reminder** | If the student stops or hesitates for 3 seconds, select *one* of the following (allowed one time):<br>—If the student has not said anything at all, provides a very limited response, or provides an off-track response, say **Tell me as much as you can about the story**.<br>—Otherwise, ask **Can you tell me anything more about the story?** |
| **Discontinue** | After the first reminder, if the student does not say anything or gets off track for 5 seconds, say **Thank you** and discontinue the task. |

DORF/Level 2

# Going to School

▶ How do you get to school? Do you ride a school bus or travel by car? Do you ride a bike or walk? Do you think about how children around the world get to school? Some children arrive at school just like you do. Others have a very different journey.

Like American children, many students around the world walk to school. However, it may take them an hour or more to get there. Then they make the same walk home when school is over.

Do you know anyone who travels to school in a boat? Some children live in fishing villages. Their school is a large houseboat in the middle of a river or other waterway.

There are families around the world who travel from place to place following cattle they own. Many of these people use camels to move from place to place. For many of these children, their school and their teacher travel with them. The children learn while they travel.

Some children live on mountains. There may not be a school nearby. These children do not travel to school at all. Instead, school comes to them on a radio. They do not hear music over the airwaves. They hear lessons in math and other school subjects.

The next time you travel to school, think about other children around the world. What would it be like to go to school in a different way?

# 15 DIBELS® Oral Reading Fluency
Level 2/Progress Monitoring 15

Read the directions on page 171.

▶ **Begin testing. *Put your finger under the first word*** (point to the first word of the passage)*. **Ready, begin.***

| | |
|---|---|
| *Timing* | 1 minute. Start your stopwatch after the student says the first word of the passage. Place a bracket ( **]** ) and say ***Stop*** after 1 minute. |
| *Wait* | If no response in 3 seconds, say the word and mark it as incorrect. |
| *Discontinue* | If no words are read correctly in the first line, say ***Stop***, record a score of 0, and do not administer Retell. |
| | If fewer than 40 words are read correctly on any passage, use professional judgment whether to administer Retell for that passage. |
| *Reminders* | If the student stops (and it's not a hesitation on a specific item), say ***Keep going.*** (Repeat as often as needed.) |
| | If the student loses her/his place, point. (Repeat as often as needed.) |

# 15 DIBELS® Oral Reading Fluency
Level 2/Progress Monitoring 15 Retell

▶ *Now tell me as much as you can about the story you just read. Ready, begin.*

| | |
|---|---|
| *Timing* | 1-minute maximum. Start your stopwatch after telling the student to begin. Say **Stop** after 1 minute. |
| *Wait/ Reminder* | If the student stops or hesitates for 3 seconds, select *one* of the following (allowed one time): <br> —If the student has not said anything at all, provides a very limited response, or provides an off-track response, say **Tell me as much as you can about the story**. <br> —Otherwise, ask **Can you tell me anything more about the story?** |
| *Discontinue* | After the first reminder, if the student does not say anything or gets off track for 5 seconds, say **Thank you** and discontinue the task. |

# A Happy House Plant

▶ Do you have plants in your home? There are many reasons why you should. Plants improve the air in your home. They also make your home look more inviting. In addition, many people enjoy taking care of plants in their home. It can be a great way to relax!

If you have decided to put a plant in your home, the first thing to do is decide what kind of plant to buy. If you go to a plant store, you will find many different kinds of plants to choose from. Many people choose a spider plant.

You can probably guess what a spider plant looks like. The plants often grow in hanging baskets. They have green stalks that grow quite long, past the bottom of the container. Eventually, small plants will begin to grow at the ends of the stalks. The small plants look like spiders. If you cut off the small plants and place them in fertile soil, they will grow into new spider plants.

Spider plants are easy to care for. They need to be planted in a rich soil. Make sure the container has small holes in the bottom. When you water the plant, the holes let the extra water drain out. Spider plants do not like to sit and grow in wet soil! The soil should feel dry before you

# 16 DIBELS® Oral Reading Fluency
Level 2/Progress Monitoring 16

Read the directions on page 171.

▶ Begin testing. *Put your finger under the first word* (point to the first word of the passage). *Ready, begin.*

| | |
|---|---|
| *Timing* | 1 minute. Start your stopwatch after the student says the first word of the passage. Place a bracket ( ] ) and say *Stop* after 1 minute. |
| *Wait* | If no response in 3 seconds, say the word and mark it as incorrect. |
| *Discontinue* | If no words are read correctly in the first line, say *Stop*, record a score of 0, and do not administer Retell. |
| | If fewer than 40 words are read correctly on any passage, use professional judgment whether to administer Retell for that passage. |
| *Reminders* | If the student stops (and it's not a hesitation on a specific item), say *Keep going.* (Repeat as often as needed.) |
| | If the student loses her/his place, point. (Repeat as often as needed.) |
| *Turn page* | If student reaches the end of the page (designated by triangles in the scoring booklet) before the minute is up, turn the page and continue on the next page. Otherwise, proceed to Retell when the minute is up. |

# A Happy House Plant

give the plant more water. A spider plant grows well in almost any kind of light. Keep it in a warm place, too. If you follow these tips, you will likely have a wonderful houseplant to enjoy for a long time.

DORF/Level 2

# 16 DIBELS® Oral Reading Fluency
Level 2/Progress Monitoring 16 Retell

▶ *Now tell me as much as you can about the story you just read. Ready, begin.*

| | |
|---|---|
| *Timing* | 1-minute maximum. Start your stopwatch after telling the student to begin. Say **Stop** after 1 minute. |
| *Wait/ Reminder* | If the student stops or hesitates for 3 seconds, select *one* of the following (allowed one time):<br>—If the student has not said anything at all, provides a very limited response, or provides an off-track response, say **Tell me as much as you can about the story**.<br>—Otherwise, ask **Can you tell me anything more about the story?** |
| *Discontinue* | After the first reminder, if the student does not say anything or gets off track for 5 seconds, say **Thank you** and discontinue the task. |

DORF/Level 2

# A Gift of Chores

▶ For a week, Will and Max had been talking about how to celebrate Mom's birthday. The brothers had many grand ideas, such as buying Mom a ring or sending her on a trip. However, there was one problem. The boys did not have any money. What could they possibly give Mom that did not cost a lot?

Finally, at dinner, Will and Max had an idea. It happened just after the family finished eating. The boys cleared the table as they always do. Mom began washing the dishes. As she did, she let out a huge sigh and said she wished the dishes would wash themselves. Will and Max looked at each other. They both had the same great idea! They would make a chore coupon book for Mom.

First, the brothers made a list of chores such as washing the dog and taking out the trash. Then they began making coupons from colored paper. They cut pieces of paper in the size of dollar bills. Each boy made five coupons for chores and a cover for the book. Then they stapled them all together and wrapped the book.

The next morning, the boys gave Mom her present. She opened it and read the cover. She flipped through the coupons. She exclaimed, "This is the best present anyone has ever given me!" The boys felt happy and proud.

# 17 DIBELS® Oral Reading Fluency
Level 2/Progress Monitoring 17

Read the directions on page 171.

▶ Begin testing. *Put your finger under the first word* (point to the first word of the passage). *Ready, begin.*

| | |
|---|---|
| *Timing* | 1 minute. Start your stopwatch after the student says the first word of the passage. Place a bracket ( **]** ) and say *Stop* after 1 minute. |
| *Wait* | If no response in 3 seconds, say the word and mark it as incorrect. |
| *Discontinue* | If no words are read correctly in the first line, say *Stop*, record a score of 0, and do not administer Retell. |
| | If fewer than 40 words are read correctly on any passage, use professional judgment whether to administer Retell for that passage. |
| *Reminders* | If the student stops (and it's not a hesitation on a specific item), say *Keep going.* (Repeat as often as needed.) |
| | If the student loses her/his place, point. (Repeat as often as needed.) |

# 17 DIBELS® Oral Reading Fluency
Level 2/Progress Monitoring 17 Retell

▶ *Now tell me as much as you can about the story you just read. Ready, begin.*

| | |
|---|---|
| *Timing* | 1-minute maximum. Start your stopwatch after telling the student to begin. Say **Stop** after 1 minute. |
| *Wait/ Reminder* | If the student stops or hesitates for 3 seconds, select *one* of the following (allowed one time):<br>—If the student has not said anything at all, provides a very limited response, or provides an off-track response, say **Tell me as much as you can about the story**.<br>—Otherwise, ask **Can you tell me anything more about the story?** |
| *Discontinue* | After the first reminder, if the student does not say anything or gets off track for 5 seconds, say **Thank you** and discontinue the task. |

## Canoe Fun

▶ The summer sun was shining and there were no clouds in the sky. It was a perfect day to try out our new canoe at the lake. We put the canoe in the water close to the shore and put on our life jackets. Then we grabbed the paddles and got into the canoe.

I had never been in a canoe, and I had a lot to learn about how to paddle one. The most difficult part was paddling in a straight line. My seat was in the middle of the canoe. I paddled until I got tired. Then Mom and Dad let me rest.

As the canoe skimmed along the water, there was a lot to see. I counted leaves that were floating in the water. I saw a turtle sunning himself on a rock. We all laughed when a fish jumped out of the water directly in front of the canoe. "Look!" said Dad suddenly. We followed his pointing finger and saw a golden eagle sitting in the top of a tall tree.

We were all so busy paddling and enjoying the sights that we didn't notice the clouds forming. "Looks like it might rain," said Dad. "We better head back to shore." We turned around and paddled hard. On the way back, I didn't take a rest, even though I was tired.

We reached the shore and got out of the canoe. As soon as we got in the car, the first raindrops started to fall. We all cheered. We had made it back just in time.

# 18 DIBELS® Oral Reading Fluency
Level 2/Progress Monitoring 18

Read the directions on page 171.

▶ **Begin testing.** *Put your finger under the first word* (point to the first word of the passage). *Ready, begin.*

---

| | |
|---|---|
| *Timing* | 1 minute. Start your stopwatch after the student says the first word of the passage. Place a bracket ( **]** ) and say *Stop* after 1 minute. |
| *Wait* | If no response in 3 seconds, say the word and mark it as incorrect. |
| *Discontinue* | If no words are read correctly in the first line, say *Stop*, record a score of 0, and do not administer Retell.<br><br>If fewer than 40 words are read correctly on any passage, use professional judgment whether to administer Retell for that passage. |
| *Reminders* | If the student stops (and it's not a hesitation on a specific item), say *Keep going.* (Repeat as often as needed.)<br><br>If the student loses her/his place, point. (Repeat as often as needed.) |

# 18 DIBELS® Oral Reading Fluency
Level 2/Progress Monitoring 18 Retell

▶ *Now tell me as much as you can about the story you just read. Ready, begin.*

| | |
|---|---|
| **Timing** | 1-minute maximum. Start your stopwatch after telling the student to begin. Say **Stop** after 1 minute. |
| **Wait/ Reminder** | If the student stops or hesitates for 3 seconds, select *one* of the following (allowed one time):<br>—If the student has not said anything at all, provides a very limited response, or provides an off-track response, say **Tell me as much as you can about the story**.<br>—Otherwise, ask **Can you tell me anything more about the story?** |
| **Discontinue** | After the first reminder, if the student does not say anything or gets off track for 5 seconds, say **Thank you** and discontinue the task. |

# African Drums

▶ When you listen to a song, what do you hear? Many people enjoy the beat of the drum. In Africa, drums are important. They are used in music, but they are also used to talk to people.

There are many different types of African drums. They come in all shapes and sizes and each one makes a special sound. Some African drums have an animal skin stretched across a wood base. People hit the skin with their hand or with a stick to make sound. Other African drums are logs with slits carved in them. People hit the slits or scrape a stick over them to make sound. A third type of African drum is like a rattle. People shake it to make sound.

In some parts of Africa, people use talking drums. These drums do not really talk, but their beats give a message. One drum beat is used when a baby is born. People hear the drum beat and know that a new baby has come into the world. Other drum beats say that someone is visiting or that two people have gotten married. Many people might drum the rhythms at the same time.

African drums are also used to celebrate special events. Dancers often do a certain dance for each event. The dancers may wear rattles on their wrists and ankles. As they dance, the rattles make noises that

# 19 DIBELS® Oral Reading Fluency
Level 2/Progress Monitoring 19

Read the directions on page 171.

▶ **Begin testing. *Put your finger under the first word*** (point to the first word of the passage). ***Ready, begin.***

| | |
|---|---|
| *Timing* | 1 minute. Start your stopwatch after the student says the first word of the passage. Place a bracket ( **]** ) and say ***Stop*** after 1 minute. |
| *Wait* | If no response in 3 seconds, say the word and mark it as incorrect. |
| *Discontinue* | If no words are read correctly in the first line, say ***Stop***, record a score of 0, and do not administer Retell. |
| | If fewer than 40 words are read correctly on any passage, use professional judgment whether to administer Retell for that passage. |
| *Reminders* | If the student stops (and it's not a hesitation on a specific item), say ***Keep going.*** (Repeat as often as needed.) |
| | If the student loses her/his place, point. (Repeat as often as needed.) |
| *Turn page* | If student reaches the end of the page (designated by triangles in the scoring booklet) before the minute is up, turn the page and continue on the next page. Otherwise, proceed to Retell when the minute is up. |

## African Drums

add to the sound of the drum beat.

   While you may enjoy the sound of African drums, their beats also mean many things.

---

DORF/Level 2

# 19 DIBELS® Oral Reading Fluency
Level 2/Progress Monitoring 19 Retell

▶ *Now tell me as much as you can about the story you just read. Ready, begin.*

| | |
|---|---|
| *Timing* | 1-minute maximum. Start your stopwatch after telling the student to begin. Say **Stop** after 1 minute. |
| *Wait/ Reminder* | If the student stops or hesitates for 3 seconds, select *one* of the following (allowed one time):<br>—If the student has not said anything at all, provides a very limited response, or provides an off-track response, say **Tell me as much as you can about the story**.<br>—Otherwise, ask **Can you tell me anything more about the story?** |
| *Discontinue* | After the first reminder, if the student does not say anything or gets off track for 5 seconds, say **Thank you** and discontinue the task. |

# Flower Parts

▶ Many people enjoy flowers in outdoor gardens and in vases in their homes. Flowers come in all colors and sizes, and many flowers smell pleasant. People buy roses for their sweet smell and beautiful color. A rose may be red and small enough to hold in your hand. A sunflower may be yellow and tower over your head. One kind of flower smells so bad, many people hold their nose when they walk by!

Flowers are not just for us to enjoy. They have a job to do. Flowers make seeds for the plant. When the seeds are released, they grow into new plants.

While there are many different kinds of flowers, they all have some parts in common. Most flowers have petals. Petals are the colorful parts we admire. Petals attract insects to the flower. Insects follow the petals to get nectar. Nectar is a rich food for the insects. The nectar is at the bottom of the petals.

When an insect lands on the petals to get nectar, it also touches the stamens. These flower parts stick up inside the flower. Their tips are usually yellow and have pollen on them. As the insect gets nectar, pollen sticks to its body. When the insect goes to another flower for more nectar, it takes the pollen with it.

# 20 DIBELS® Oral Reading Fluency
Level 2/Progress Monitoring 20

Read the directions on page 171.

▶ **Begin testing. *Put your finger under the first word*** (point to the first word of the passage). ***Ready, begin.***

| | |
|---|---|
| *Timing* | 1 minute. Start your stopwatch after the student says the first word of the passage. Place a bracket ( **]** ) and say ***Stop*** after 1 minute. |
| *Wait* | If no response in 3 seconds, say the word and mark it as incorrect. |
| *Discontinue* | If no words are read correctly in the first line, say ***Stop***, record a score of 0, and do not administer Retell. |
| | If fewer than 40 words are read correctly on any passage, use professional judgment whether to administer Retell for that passage. |
| *Reminders* | If the student stops (and it's not a hesitation on a specific item), say ***Keep going.*** (Repeat as often as needed.) |
| | If the student loses her/his place, point. (Repeat as often as needed.) |
| *Turn page* | If student reaches the end of the page (designated by triangles in the scoring booklet) before the minute is up, turn the page and continue on the next page. Otherwise, proceed to Retell when the minute is up. |

DORF/Level 2

## Flower Parts

At the other flower, the insect will land on the petals. Some of the pollen it carries will come off on the other flower. Now this flower will begin to make seeds. The seeds will one day grow more plants that will make more flowers. Through this process, flowers will continue to grow and bloom.

DORF/Level 2

# 20 DIBELS® Oral Reading Fluency
Level 2/Progress Monitoring 20 Retell

▶ *Now tell me as much as you can about the story you just read. Ready, begin.*

| | |
|---|---|
| **Timing** | 1-minute maximum. Start your stopwatch after telling the student to begin. Say **Stop** after 1 minute. |
| **Wait/ Reminder** | If the student stops or hesitates for 3 seconds, select *one* of the following (allowed one time):<br>—If the student has not said anything at all, provides a very limited response, or provides an off-track response, say **Tell me as much as you can about the story**.<br>—Otherwise, ask **Can you tell me anything more about the story?** |
| **Discontinue** | After the first reminder, if the student does not say anything or gets off track for 5 seconds, say **Thank you** and discontinue the task. |

DORF/Level 2

## DIBELS® Oral Reading Fluency
Level 3/Progress Monitoring

*Directions:* Make sure you have reviewed the scoring rules in the *DIBELS Next Assessment Manual* and have them available. Say these specific directions to the student:

▶ *I would like you to read a story to me. Please do your best reading. If you do not know a word, I will read the word for you. Keep reading until I say "stop." Be ready to tell me all about the story when you finish.*

▶ **Go to the next Progress Monitoring passage in the sequence.**

# A New Ball Game

▶ On the first day of school, Roy's teacher asked him to write a letter about himself. Roy was glad to have the chance to talk about his life in Africa. Roy had been born in the United States, but his family had lived in a small town in Africa for three years. Now his family had moved back to the United States.

Roy's stepmom was a doctor. She worked in a clinic, where she treated sick people and gave immunizations. His dad taught music at the school Roy and his brother attended. Roy and his friends played sports together and practiced playing the instruments his dad taught them. Football was his favorite sport and there always seemed to be a game going after school.

In his letter, Roy wrote about his life and that he missed playing football the most. He had seen American football and it was a very different game. It was hard to figure out why they were chasing each other and when to cheer.

He handed the letter to his teacher the next morning. That afternoon as he was leaving, his teacher called him over. Another boy was standing next to her. "Roy, this is Spencer," his teacher said. "He's going to

# 1 DIBELS® Oral Reading Fluency
Level 3/Progress Monitoring 1

Read the directions on page 273.

▶ Begin testing. *Put your finger under the first word* (point to the first word of the passage). *Ready, begin.*

| | |
|---|---|
| *Timing* | 1 minute. Start your stopwatch after the student says the first word of the passage. Place a bracket ( **]** ) and say *Stop* after 1 minute. |
| *Wait* | If no response in 3 seconds, say the word and mark it as incorrect. |
| *Discontinue* | If no words are read correctly in the first line, say *Stop*, record a score of 0, and do not administer Retell.<br><br>If fewer than 40 words are read correctly on any passage, use professional judgment whether to administer Retell for that passage. |
| *Reminders* | If the student stops (and it's not a hesitation on a specific item), say *Keep going.* (Repeat as often as needed.)<br><br>If the student loses her/his place, point. (Repeat as often as needed.) |
| *Turn page* | If student reaches the end of the page (designated by triangles in the scoring booklet) before the minute is up, turn the page and continue on the next page. Otherwise, proceed to Retell when the minute is up. |

## A New Ball Game

introduce you to the soccer team. I think you'll enjoy it."

Spencer smiled at Roy and led him outside to the field, where a group of kids were playing. "The teacher said you call this football in Africa, but here it's called soccer," said Spencer. Roy looked around. The kids were playing the same game he had played back in Africa! He couldn't wait to join them.

# 1 DIBELS® Oral Reading Fluency
Level 3/Progress Monitoring 1 Retell

▶ *Now tell me as much as you can about the story you just read. Ready, begin.*

| | |
|---|---|
| **Timing** | 1-minute maximum. Start your stopwatch after telling the student to begin. Say **Stop** after 1 minute. |
| **Wait/ Reminder** | If the student stops or hesitates for 3 seconds, select *one* of the following (allowed one time):<br>—If the student has not said anything at all, provides a very limited response, or provides an off-track response, say **Tell me as much as you can about the story**.<br>—Otherwise, ask **Can you tell me anything more about the story?** |
| **Discontinue** | After the first reminder, if the student does not say anything or gets off track for 5 seconds, say **Thank you** and discontinue the task. |

# Swimming the Channel

▶ In the sport of swimming, people have set many types of records. Some records are for speed or distance. Other records are for swimming across difficult waters. The English Channel swim is one of these. Many people have dreamed about swimming across this stretch of water, but very few have done it. Lynne Cox is one of the few.

The English Channel is between the French and English coasts. At its shortest point, the distance across it is twenty-two miles, but the water is so cold and the currents so strong that only ten percent of those who have tried the swim have made it across. The first swimmer to do so was a man named Matthew Webb. He made the swim in 1875, and it took him more than twenty hours.

Lynne Cox first swam across the Channel in 1972. She had started swimming at the age of three in Maine, but it wasn't until her family moved to California that Lynne discovered her love of swimming in open water. It was then that Lynne knew she wanted to swim the Channel. At age fifteen, Lynne was the youngest person ever to attempt the swim. She made it across in less than ten hours, which at that time was faster than any other man or woman had ever done it. This first swim covered

# 2 DIBELS® Oral Reading Fluency
Level 3/Progress Monitoring 2

Read the directions on page 273.

▶ **Begin testing. *Put your finger under the first word*** (point to the first word of the passage). ***Ready, begin.***

| | |
|---|---|
| *Timing* | 1 minute. Start your stopwatch after the student says the first word of the passage. Place a bracket ( ] ) and say ***Stop*** after 1 minute. |
| *Wait* | If no response in 3 seconds, say the word and mark it as incorrect. |
| *Discontinue* | If no words are read correctly in the first line, say ***Stop***, record a score of 0, and do not administer Retell. |
| | If fewer than 40 words are read correctly on any passage, use professional judgment whether to administer Retell for that passage. |
| *Reminders* | If the student stops (and it's not a hesitation on a specific item), say ***Keep going.*** (Repeat as often as needed.) |
| | If the student loses her/his place, point. (Repeat as often as needed.) |
| *Turn page* | If student reaches the end of the page (designated by triangles in the scoring booklet) before the minute is up, turn the page and continue on the next page. Otherwise, proceed to Retell when the minute is up. |

**DORF/Level 3**

## Swimming the Channel

a stretch of twenty-seven miles. The next year, Lynne returned and broke her own record. She swam a thirty-three mile stretch of the Channel in nine hours and thirty-six minutes.

## 2 DIBELS® Oral Reading Fluency
Level 3/Progress Monitoring 2 Retell

▶ *Now tell me as much as you can about the story you just read. Ready, begin.*

| | |
|---|---|
| ***Timing*** | 1-minute maximum. Start your stopwatch after telling the student to begin. Say **Stop** after 1 minute. |
| ***Wait/ Reminder*** | If the student stops or hesitates for 3 seconds, select *one* of the following (allowed one time): <br> —If the student has not said anything at all, provides a very limited response, or provides an off-track response, say **Tell me as much as you can about the story**. <br> —Otherwise, ask **Can you tell me anything more about the story?** |
| ***Discontinue*** | After the first reminder, if the student does not say anything or gets off track for 5 seconds, say **Thank you** and discontinue the task. |

# Rooftop Gardens

▶ What do you think of when you hear the word "garden"? Maybe you have planted a garden at home. Many schools also have gardens that students can work in. Most people think about gardens being planted in the ground, but there are many other places to plant gardens. One good place for a garden is on the roof!

A rooftop garden, or a "green roof," can be planted on top of a small house or on a giant skyscraper. Almost any type of roof can have some type of garden or green space. Even steep roofs can have a patch of grass for wild flowers.

You might ask, "Why put a garden on the roof?" Roof gardens do more than add spots of beauty to our rooftops. They are a good way to help the environment in areas that are covered with concrete sidewalks and paved streets.

Green roofs also provide insulation. They keep buildings cooler in the summer and warmer in the winter. This saves energy and reduces the amount of fuel we use. Rooftop gardens also help stop pollution. The gardens soak up rainwater that would otherwise run off onto dirty streets and roads. Less dirty water is able to pollute our rivers and streams.

# 3 DIBELS® Oral Reading Fluency
Level 3/Progress Monitoring 3

Read the directions on page 273.

▶ **Begin testing. *Put your finger under the first word*** (point to the first word of the passage). ***Ready, begin.***

| | |
|---|---|
| *Timing* | 1 minute. Start your stopwatch after the student says the first word of the passage. Place a bracket ( ] ) and say ***Stop*** after 1 minute. |
| *Wait* | If no response in 3 seconds, say the word and mark it as incorrect. |
| *Discontinue* | If no words are read correctly in the first line, say ***Stop***, record a score of 0, and do not administer Retell.<br><br>If fewer than 40 words are read correctly on any passage, use professional judgment whether to administer Retell for that passage. |
| *Reminders* | If the student stops (and it's not a hesitation on a specific item), say ***Keep going.*** (Repeat as often as needed.)<br><br>If the student loses her/his place, point. (Repeat as often as needed.) |
| *Turn page* | If student reaches the end of the page (designated by triangles in the scoring booklet) before the minute is up, turn the page and continue on the next page. Otherwise, proceed to Retell when the minute is up. |

## Rooftop Gardens

Another great thing about rooftop gardens is that they offer a natural place for birds to nest and live. Birds that normally would not be able to find food or a safe place to nest in cities can live happily in rooftop gardens.

As you can see, rooftop gardens can be a good addition to any building. So, the next time you think about a garden, don't just look down at the ground. Look up at the rooftops!

# 3 DIBELS® Oral Reading Fluency
Level 3/Progress Monitoring 3 Retell

▶ *Now tell me as much as you can about the story you just read. Ready, begin.*

| | |
|---|---|
| *Timing* | 1-minute maximum. Start your stopwatch after telling the student to begin. Say **Stop** after 1 minute. |
| *Wait/ Reminder* | If the student stops or hesitates for 3 seconds, select *one* of the following (allowed one time):<br>—If the student has not said anything at all, provides a very limited response, or provides an off-track response, say **Tell me as much as you can about the story**.<br>—Otherwise, ask **Can you tell me anything more about the story?** |
| *Discontinue* | After the first reminder, if the student does not say anything or gets off track for 5 seconds, say **Thank you** and discontinue the task. |

# Learning to Skateboard

▶ The last box was finally unpacked at the new house. Zach had been excited about moving to the city and about making new friends. He knew he had several weeks to explore the neighborhood before school started, and he realized that was plenty of time to learn his way around. He asked his mom if he could walk to the nearby park.

From the road, the park looked like a giant green expanse. Now, he saw that it was divided into different sections. The first thing that caught his eye was the skate park. He sprinted to the gate and stood looking in at the ramps and rails. He had a skateboard but had never learned to ride it. The roads near his old house had been too rocky.

Just then, two boys zoomed up on skateboards and said hello. They asked him if he skateboarded. He told them that he had a board but had never had a place to learn. "Well, now you do," they said, and they offered to teach him. Their names were Matt and Pablo, and they went to the same school he was going to attend. Zach happily agreed to meet them for a lesson.

The following afternoon, Zach went to find the boys. After putting on helmets and pads, Matt showed him how to stand on the board above

# 4 DIBELS® Oral Reading Fluency
Level 3/Progress Monitoring 4

Read the directions on page 273.

▶ **Begin testing.** *Put your finger under the first word* (point to the first word of the passage). *Ready, begin.*

| | |
|---|---|
| *Timing* | 1 minute. Start your stopwatch after the student says the first word of the passage. Place a bracket ( ] ) and say *Stop* after 1 minute. |
| *Wait* | If no response in 3 seconds, say the word and mark it as incorrect. |
| *Discontinue* | If no words are read correctly in the first line, say *Stop*, record a score of 0, and do not administer Retell. |
| | If fewer than 40 words are read correctly on any passage, use professional judgment whether to administer Retell for that passage. |
| *Reminders* | If the student stops (and it's not a hesitation on a specific item), say *Keep going.* (Repeat as often as needed.) |
| | If the student loses her/his place, point. (Repeat as often as needed.) |
| *Turn page* | If student reaches the end of the page (designated by triangles in the scoring booklet) before the minute is up, turn the page and continue on the next page. Otherwise, proceed to Retell when the minute is up. |

## Learning to Skateboard

the axle. Pablo helped him practice pushing off, which is the movement needed to get the board rolling. They also explained carving and stopping. Zach practiced and also watched the other guys perform some advanced moves they had mastered. After thanking his new friends, he promised to come back every day. By the time school started, he had learned to skateboard and had made two good friends.

## 4 DIBELS® Oral Reading Fluency
Level 3/Progress Monitoring 4 Retell

▶ *Now tell me as much as you can about the story you just read. Ready, begin.*

| | |
|---|---|
| **Timing** | 1-minute maximum. Start your stopwatch after telling the student to begin. Say **Stop** after 1 minute. |
| **Wait/ Reminder** | If the student stops or hesitates for 3 seconds, select *one* of the following (allowed one time):<br>—If the student has not said anything at all, provides a very limited response, or provides an off-track response, say **Tell me as much as you can about the story**.<br>—Otherwise, ask **Can you tell me anything more about the story?** |
| **Discontinue** | After the first reminder, if the student does not say anything or gets off track for 5 seconds, say **Thank you** and discontinue the task. |

# Glassmaking

▶ The morning sun came in the window, sending a rainbow of color dancing around the room. Jayden sat in Gran's kitchen gazing at the glass vases that sat on shelves in front of the window. Her grandmother had collected them from all over the world. Jayden loved that each piece was different. Each time she visited, she saw some new detail that she had missed before.

Jayden asked her grandmother how the glass was made. Gran started explaining, but then she stopped. "I know," she said. "Let's visit my friend Mary's studio and you can see for yourself."

At the glass studio, Mary showed them how glass was blown. She explained that sand and other ingredients are mixed together and put into a very hot furnace to form molten glass. They watched as Mary dipped the tip of her blowpipe into the furnace and scooped some glass onto the end. Carefully, she rolled the hot glass back and forth on a steel table, forming a neat ball. Then she blew into the pipe to form an air bubble inside the glass. She said that as the glass cooled, it had to be reheated to keep it soft enough to work with. Jayden watched closely as Mary placed the pipe back into the furnace.

# 5 DIBELS® Oral Reading Fluency
Level 3/Progress Monitoring 5

Read the directions on page 273.

▶ **Begin testing.** *Put your finger under the first word* (point to the first word of the passage). *Ready, begin.*

| | |
|---|---|
| *Timing* | 1 minute. Start your stopwatch after the student says the first word of the passage. Place a bracket ( ] ) and say *Stop* after 1 minute. |
| *Wait* | If no response in 3 seconds, say the word and mark it as incorrect. |
| *Discontinue* | If no words are read correctly in the first line, say *Stop*, record a score of 0, and do not administer Retell. |
| | If fewer than 40 words are read correctly on any passage, use professional judgment whether to administer Retell for that passage. |
| *Reminders* | If the student stops (and it's not a hesitation on a specific item), say *Keep going.* (Repeat as often as needed.) |
| | If the student loses her/his place, point. (Repeat as often as needed.) |
| *Turn page* | If student reaches the end of the page (designated by triangles in the scoring booklet) before the minute is up, turn the page and continue on the next page. Otherwise, proceed to Retell when the minute is up. |

## Glassmaking

While the glass heated, Mary sprinkled some blue and green colored bits across the table. Then, she rolled the reheated piece across the bits. Once again, she returned it to the furnace. This time, when she removed it, the melted color swirled inside. Jayden thought it was very beautiful. Finally, Mary shaped the form with wooden blocks and other tools before placing it in a cooling oven.

Jayden had learned so much. She thought about Gran's collection. It was now more special than ever.

DORF/Level 3

# 5 DIBELS® Oral Reading Fluency
Level 3/Progress Monitoring 5 Retell

▶ *Now tell me as much as you can about the story you just read. Ready, begin.*

| | |
|---|---|
| **Timing** | 1-minute maximum. Start your stopwatch after telling the student to begin. Say **Stop** after 1 minute. |
| **Wait/ Reminder** | If the student stops or hesitates for 3 seconds, select *one* of the following (allowed one time):<br>—If the student has not said anything at all, provides a very limited response, or provides an off-track response, say **Tell me as much as you can about the story**.<br>—Otherwise, ask **Can you tell me anything more about the story?** |
| **Discontinue** | After the first reminder, if the student does not say anything or gets off track for 5 seconds, say **Thank you** and discontinue the task. |

## Space Camp

▶ It was the summer after third grade, and Kelsey was excited. Ever since she was little, Kelsey wanted to be an astronaut. This summer she was old enough to go to space camp. For six days she would get to experience the life of an astronaut.

Kelsey would be staying at the space center with the other campers, so her father dropped her off the evening before camp began. She was so excited for the next day that she had a hard time sleeping. The next morning would begin her space adventure.

The first thing the campers did that morning was put on spacesuits. Then they went into a machine that was like a pretend rocket launch. The machine was called a simulator. The campers spent the morning practicing rocket launches and landings in the simulator. It felt like they were on a real rocket.

After lunch, it was time to divide into groups. Kelsey chose the space and aviation group because she wanted to be a pilot. She joined other campers who were interested in learning how to fly. The campers learned about the principles of flight, and they even spent time in a jet simulator.

Kelsey spent the rest of the days at camp visiting the space museum

# 6 DIBELS® Oral Reading Fluency
Level 3/Progress Monitoring 6

Read the directions on page 273.

▶ **Begin testing. *Put your finger under the first word*** (point to the first word of the passage). ***Ready, begin.***

| | |
|---|---|
| *Timing* | 1 minute. Start your stopwatch after the student says the first word of the passage. Place a bracket ( **]** ) and say ***Stop*** after 1 minute. |
| *Wait* | If no response in 3 seconds, say the word and mark it as incorrect. |
| *Discontinue* | If no words are read correctly in the first line, say ***Stop***, record a score of 0, and do not administer Retell. |
| | If fewer than 40 words are read correctly on any passage, use professional judgment whether to administer Retell for that passage. |
| *Reminders* | If the student stops (and it's not a hesitation on a specific item), say ***Keep going.*** (Repeat as often as needed.) |
| | If the student loses her/his place, point. (Repeat as often as needed.) |
| *Turn page* | If student reaches the end of the page (designated by triangles in the scoring booklet) before the minute is up, turn the page and continue on the next page. Otherwise, proceed to Retell when the minute is up. |

DORF/Level 3

## Space Camp

and climbing the rock wall that resembled Mars' surface. All of the campers had a chance to build their own rockets. At the end of the six days, the campers launched their model rockets outdoors. Kelsey felt proud as her rocket soared high in the sky. As she watched her rocket, she thought about her week at camp. Space camp was so much fun, she couldn't wait to see how much fun she would have as a real astronaut.

DORF/Level 3

# 6 DIBELS® Oral Reading Fluency
Level 3/Progress Monitoring 6 Retell

▶ *Now tell me as much as you can about the story you just read. Ready, begin.*

| | |
|---|---|
| *Timing* | 1-minute maximum. Start your stopwatch after telling the student to begin. Say **Stop** after 1 minute. |
| *Wait/ Reminder* | If the student stops or hesitates for 3 seconds, select *one* of the following (allowed one time):<br>—If the student has not said anything at all, provides a very limited response, or provides an off-track response, say **Tell me as much as you can about the story**.<br>—Otherwise, ask **Can you tell me anything more about the story?** |
| *Discontinue* | After the first reminder, if the student does not say anything or gets off track for 5 seconds, say **Thank you** and discontinue the task. |

# A Woodland Path

▶ The sun was up, and it was going to be another pretty day. Carrie was ready for the day's hike. She and her family had recently moved to a small ranch. Their land was right next to a nature preserve. Every day, Carrie and her teenage brother Jackson explored a new part of the preserve.

During the summer, Carrie and Jackson had the whole day to explore. Mom made them a lunch. Then they headed out with their cell phones, which they used to keep in touch with their parents. They carried backpacks that held their lunches and notebooks. Carrie and Jackson liked to make drawings and write about things they saw.

Carrie and her brother had already hiked many of the trails in the preserve and were hoping to find a new, special place. After walking a little way up the main path, they stopped to discuss which way to go. It was then that Carrie saw a small, overgrown path leading off to the right. She wondered how they had missed it on their earlier hikes. They were both excited at the chance to find a new part of the preserve. The path was very narrow and bushy, but they were determined to follow it to its end. Finally, after hiking for over an hour, they came upon a clearing. In

# 7 DIBELS® Oral Reading Fluency
Level 3/Progress Monitoring 7

Read the directions on page 273.

▶ **Begin testing. *Put your finger under the first word*** (point to the first word of the passage). ***Ready, begin.***

| | |
|---|---|
| *Timing* | 1 minute. Start your stopwatch after the student says the first word of the passage. Place a bracket ( **]** ) and say ***Stop*** after 1 minute. |
| *Wait* | If no response in 3 seconds, say the word and mark it as incorrect. |
| *Discontinue* | If no words are read correctly in the first line, say ***Stop***, record a score of 0, and do not administer Retell. |
| | If fewer than 40 words are read correctly on any passage, use professional judgment whether to administer Retell for that passage. |
| *Reminders* | If the student stops (and it's not a hesitation on a specific item), say ***Keep going.*** (Repeat as often as needed.) |
| | If the student loses her/his place, point. (Repeat as often as needed.) |
| *Turn page* | If student reaches the end of the page (designated by triangles in the scoring booklet) before the minute is up, turn the page and continue on the next page. Otherwise, proceed to Retell when the minute is up. |

## A Woodland Path

the clearing was the most beautiful waterfall they had ever seen. Carrie and Jackson knew that they had found a special place.

Carrie and her brother sat down by the edge of the water and took off their shoes. As they ate their lunch, they dangled their feet in the water. They were already making plans to show this special place to their parents.

# 7 DIBELS® Oral Reading Fluency
Level 3/Progress Monitoring 7 Retell

▶ *Now tell me as much as you can about the story you just read. Ready, begin.*

| | |
|---|---|
| *Timing* | 1-minute maximum. Start your stopwatch after telling the student to begin. Say **Stop** after 1 minute. |
| *Wait/ Reminder* | If the student stops or hesitates for 3 seconds, select *one* of the following (allowed one time):<br>　—If the student has not said anything at all, provides a very limited response, or provides an off-track response, say **Tell me as much as you can about the story**.<br>　—Otherwise, ask **Can you tell me anything more about the story?** |
| *Discontinue* | After the first reminder, if the student does not say anything or gets off track for 5 seconds, say **Thank you** and discontinue the task. |

## How Ryan Made a Difference

▶ One day a boy named Ryan asked his parents for seventy dollars. His teacher had explained that seventy dollars was sufficient to build a well in a poor African country. Many children in Africa were getting sick because they lacked clean water to drink. Although Ryan was only in first grade, he was determined to help them.

Ryan's parents agreed to let him do extra chores to earn the money. They would pay him one dollar per hour. He washed windows, picked up yard debris, and did other chores. In three months, Ryan had earned the seventy dollars.

When Ryan gave the money to the people who build the wells, they were grateful. They explained that the money would buy a pump to pull water from under the ground. However, it would take a lot more money to drill the well before the pump could be used. Drilling the well would cost two thousand dollars! Ryan decided to do chores until he could pay for drilling the well, too.

When the people in Ryan's town heard what he was doing, they helped him raise more money. In a few months, Ryan had enough money to pay for the well.

# 8 DIBELS® Oral Reading Fluency
Level 3/Progress Monitoring 8

▶ **Begin testing.** *Put your finger under the first word* (point to the first word of the passage). *Ready, begin.*

| | |
|---|---|
| *Timing* | 1 minute. Start your stopwatch after the student says the first word of the passage. Place a bracket ( ] ) and say *Stop* after 1 minute. |
| *Wait* | If no response in 3 seconds, say the word and mark it as incorrect. |
| *Discontinue* | If no words are read correctly in the first line, say *Stop*, record a score of 0, and do not administer Retell. |
| | If fewer than 40 words are read correctly on any passage, use professional judgment whether to administer Retell for that passage. |
| *Reminders* | If the student stops (and it's not a hesitation on a specific item), say *Keep going.* (Repeat as often as needed.) |
| | If the student loses her/his place, point. (Repeat as often as needed.) |
| *Turn page* | If student reaches the end of the page (designated by triangles in the scoring booklet) before the minute is up, turn the page and continue on the next page. Otherwise, proceed to Retell when the minute is up. |

## How Ryan Made a Difference

The well was built near a village school in Uganda. After the well was built, the villagers sent Ryan letters and a picture of the well. They had erected a sign that said "Ryan's Well." They would always remember the young person who had helped them. Ryan corresponded with the children who went to the school. Soon they became friends. Ryan was happy to think that his friends would have clean water to drink.

Ryan has continued his work. He has helped to construct wells in many African countries. He believes each individual really can make a difference.

# 8 DIBELS® Oral Reading Fluency
Level 3/Progress Monitoring 8 Retell

▶ *Now tell me as much as you can about the story you just read. Ready, begin.*

| | |
|---|---|
| *Timing* | 1-minute maximum. Start your stopwatch after telling the student to begin. Say **Stop** after 1 minute. |
| *Wait/ Reminder* | If the student stops or hesitates for 3 seconds, select *one* of the following (allowed one time):<br>—If the student has not said anything at all, provides a very limited response, or provides an off-track response, say **Tell me as much as you can about the story**.<br>—Otherwise, ask **Can you tell me anything more about the story?** |
| *Discontinue* | After the first reminder, if the student does not say anything or gets off track for 5 seconds, say **Thank you** and discontinue the task. |

## Rachel's Box

▶ The cat was making a mad dash to get away from the new puppy. She was trying to get to her spot on the window ledge out of the puppy's reach. It was then that the cat knocked over the beautiful wooden box that Grandmother had given to Rachel on her most recent visit. Steven and Rachel could see what was going to happen, but neither one was able to get across the room quickly enough to prevent it from happening.

Steven put the puppy outside while Rachel looked to see how badly the box was damaged. When he returned, his sister was still staring at the box. "Don't worry," Steven said, "It's not that serious. I think I can fix it for you." Rachel smiled happily. Her big brother was always there for her when she needed help.

They took the box to the kitchen for a closer look. The hinge needed to be screwed back on and several of the inlaid stones would have to be glued back in place. All in all, Steven thought they had been very lucky. The box was more than two hundred years old, and it had fallen on the hard floor. It had been a wedding present to their grandmother's great grandmother. For many years it had been passed down through the family to the oldest granddaughter.

# 9 DIBELS® Oral Reading Fluency
Level 3/Progress Monitoring 9

Read the directions on page 273.

▶ **Begin testing. *Put your finger under the first word*** (point to the first word of the passage). ***Ready, begin.***

| | |
|---|---|
| *Timing* | 1 minute. Start your stopwatch after the student says the first word of the passage. Place a bracket ( ] ) and say *Stop* after 1 minute. |
| *Wait* | If no response in 3 seconds, say the word and mark it as incorrect. |
| *Discontinue* | If no words are read correctly in the first line, say *Stop*, record a score of 0, and do not administer Retell. |
| | If fewer than 40 words are read correctly on any passage, use professional judgment whether to administer Retell for that passage. |
| *Reminders* | If the student stops (and it's not a hesitation on a specific item), say *Keep going.* (Repeat as often as needed.) |
| | If the student loses her/his place, point. (Repeat as often as needed.) |
| *Turn page* | If student reaches the end of the page (designated by triangles in the scoring booklet) before the minute is up, turn the page and continue on the next page. Otherwise, proceed to Retell when the minute is up. |

## Rachel's Box

The brother and sister worked together, and soon the box was as good as new. Rachel put the box in her glass cabinet. She didn't want the cat to get anywhere near it again. Because of Steven's help, she knew she would now be able to keep the box safe to give to her own granddaughter some day. Rachel felt thankful to have such a wonderful brother.

# 9 DIBELS® Oral Reading Fluency
Level 3/Progress Monitoring 9 Retell

▶ *Now tell me as much as you can about the story you just read. Ready, begin.*

| | |
|---|---|
| *Timing* | 1-minute maximum. Start your stopwatch after telling the student to begin. Say **Stop** after 1 minute. |
| *Wait/ Reminder* | If the student stops or hesitates for 3 seconds, select *one* of the following (allowed one time):<br>—If the student has not said anything at all, provides a very limited response, or provides an off-track response, say **Tell me as much as you can about the story**.<br>—Otherwise, ask **Can you tell me anything more about the story?** |
| *Discontinue* | After the first reminder, if the student does not say anything or gets off track for 5 seconds, say **Thank you** and discontinue the task. |

DORF/Level 3

# The Pinecone Feast

▶  Snow had covered the ground for a full month now. Somehow, it seemed colder than in years past. Oscar hadn't seen many birds at all. He looked out of the window and wondered how all the birds stayed warm and what they ate during these cold frosty months. His grandfather looked up from the book he was reading and asked what Oscar was so concerned about.

Oscar told him he was worried about the birds in the cold. Grandfather told him that many birds flew south for the winter but that the birds that stayed probably did need food. Then, Grandfather smiled and said, "I used to make pinecone feasts for the birds during the winter. Would you like me to show you how?" Oscar nodded an excited yes.

Oscar followed Grandfather out to the shed to retrieve some pinecones they had gathered in the fall. At the kitchen table, they carefully tied string around the top of each one. Next, Grandfather got out a jar of peanut butter and two spoons. He told Oscar to cover each pinecone with peanut butter. Then, Grandfather poured some birdseed onto a plate. He added sunflower seeds and dried fruit to the mix to give the birds extra energy. Finally, the two rolled the coated pinecones

# 10 DIBELS® Oral Reading Fluency
Level 3/Progress Monitoring 10

Read the directions on page 273.

▶ **Begin testing. *Put your finger under the first word*** (point to the first word of the passage). ***Ready, begin.***

| | |
|---|---|
| *Timing* | 1 minute. Start your stopwatch after the student says the first word of the passage. Place a bracket ( **]** ) and say ***Stop*** after 1 minute. |
| *Wait* | If no response in 3 seconds, say the word and mark it as incorrect. |
| *Discontinue* | If no words are read correctly in the first line, say ***Stop***, record a score of 0, and do not administer Retell. |
| | If fewer than 40 words are read correctly on any passage, use professional judgment whether to administer Retell for that passage. |
| *Reminders* | If the student stops (and it's not a hesitation on a specific item), say ***Keep going.*** (Repeat as often as needed.) |
| | If the student loses her/his place, point. (Repeat as often as needed.) |
| *Turn page* | If student reaches the end of the page (designated by triangles in the scoring booklet) before the minute is up, turn the page and continue on the next page. Otherwise, proceed to Retell when the minute is up. |

**DORF/Level 3**

## The Pinecone Feast

through the birdseed until they were completely covered with seeds.

Oscar and Grandfather dressed warmly and went out to set up the bird feast. They carefully tied each pinecone onto the bare branches of the big tree outside the kitchen window. After a quick snowball fight, they went inside to get warm and wait for the birds to find the feast. By lunchtime, Oscar and Grandfather had their reward. They looked out the window. There was a group of birds happily munching on the seeds.

---

DORF/Level 3

# 10 DIBELS® Oral Reading Fluency
Level 3/Progress Monitoring 10 Retell

▶ *Now tell me as much as you can about the story you just read. Ready, begin.*

| | |
|---|---|
| *Timing* | 1-minute maximum. Start your stopwatch after telling the student to begin. Say **Stop** after 1 minute. |
| *Wait/ Reminder* | If the student stops or hesitates for 3 seconds, select *one* of the following (allowed one time): <br> —If the student has not said anything at all, provides a very limited response, or provides an off-track response, say *Tell me as much as you can about the story*. <br> —Otherwise, ask *Can you tell me anything more about the story?* |
| *Discontinue* | After the first reminder, if the student does not say anything or gets off track for 5 seconds, say **Thank you** and discontinue the task. |

## Save the Turtles!

► For millions of years, sea turtles have lived in our oceans. It is amazing, when you think about it. They were here when the dinosaurs walked the Earth! Now, their future is at risk. The good news is that efforts are being made to keep all sea turtles safe.

Of the seven species of sea turtles, the largest is the leatherback. This turtle can grow to over six feet long. They are called leatherbacks because they have a softer, more flexible shell than other turtles. They live mainly in the open ocean, where they feed on jellyfish. Because they can keep their body temperature warmer than that of the water, they are able to swim in colder parts of the ocean. Other types of sea turtles are not able to do this. Leatherbacks swim thousands of miles a year looking for food. Every two or three years, the females walk onto the beach to make a nest and lay their eggs.

Each year, there are fewer nesting leatherbacks to be seen. This is because of the growing dangers they face. At sea, this giant turtle often gets caught in fishing nets. On land, animals and people disturb their nests. The turtles also mistake plastic bags and other kinds of trash for jellyfish. These bags can be very harmful to the turtles if they try to eat

# 11 DIBELS® Oral Reading Fluency
Level 3/Progress Monitoring 11

Read the directions on page 273.

▶ Begin testing. *Put your finger under the first word* (point to the first word of the passage). *Ready, begin.*

| | |
|---|---|
| *Timing* | 1 minute. Start your stopwatch after the student says the first word of the passage. Place a bracket ( **]** ) and say *Stop* after 1 minute. |
| *Wait* | If no response in 3 seconds, say the word and mark it as incorrect. |
| *Discontinue* | If no words are read correctly in the first line, say *Stop*, record a score of 0, and do not administer Retell. |
| | If fewer than 40 words are read correctly on any passage, use professional judgment whether to administer Retell for that passage. |
| *Reminders* | If the student stops (and it's not a hesitation on a specific item), say *Keep going.* (Repeat as often as needed.) |
| | If the student loses her/his place, point. (Repeat as often as needed.) |
| *Turn page* | If student reaches the end of the page (designated by triangles in the scoring booklet) before the minute is up, turn the page and continue on the next page. Otherwise, proceed to Retell when the minute is up. |

DORF/Level 3

# Save the Turtles!

them.

    Laws are being passed to protect the turtles, and people are becoming better aware of the risks. Many countries now have beach patrols to guard the nests, and there are new ways to track where the turtles go. Also, more people recycle now. This means that people throw away fewer plastic bags. If we all work together, we can save the turtles!

DORF/Level 3

## 11 DIBELS® Oral Reading Fluency
Level 3/Progress Monitoring 11 Retell

▶ *Now tell me as much as you can about the story you just read. Ready, begin.*

| | |
|---|---|
| *Timing* | 1-minute maximum. Start your stopwatch after telling the student to begin. Say **Stop** after 1 minute. |
| *Wait/ Reminder* | If the student stops or hesitates for 3 seconds, select *one* of the following (allowed one time): <br>—If the student has not said anything at all, provides a very limited response, or provides an off-track response, say **Tell me as much as you can about the story**. <br>—Otherwise, ask **Can you tell me anything more about the story?** |
| *Discontinue* | After the first reminder, if the student does not say anything or gets off track for 5 seconds, say **Thank you** and discontinue the task. |

DORF/Level 3

# Planting a Butterfly Garden

▶ One of the most beautiful insects on earth is the butterfly. There are thousands of different kinds of butterflies and they live in all parts of the world. In some places, though, butterflies have trouble finding the plants they need to survive. Planting a butterfly garden is a great way to help. You can both protect and enjoy the butterflies in your area.

Many parks and public gardens have whole fields planted to attract butterflies, but a butterfly garden does not have to be large. It can be a small bed in your yard or even a window box. To plan this type of garden, first find out what type of butterflies are native to where you live. Then, find out what type of plants they like. Try looking at the library or at your local garden center.

After researching local butterflies, pick a spot for your garden. Next, decide how large it will be. It can also be helpful to map out a plan for the garden. Butterflies like sunshine, so pick a sunny spot. The garden should also have some protection from the wind.

If you are planting your garden in the ground or in a raised bed, you will need to prepare the soil before putting in plants. Turn the soil to loosen it up, making sure to break up any large clumps. You can add in

# 12 DIBELS® Oral Reading Fluency
Level 3/Progress Monitoring 12

Read the directions on page 273.

▶ **Begin testing.** *Put your finger under the first word* (point to the first word of the passage). *Ready, begin.*

| | |
|---|---|
| *Timing* | 1 minute. Start your stopwatch after the student says the first word of the passage. Place a bracket ( **]** ) and say *Stop* after 1 minute. |
| *Wait* | If no response in 3 seconds, say the word and mark it as incorrect. |
| *Discontinue* | If no words are read correctly in the first line, say *Stop*, record a score of 0, and do not administer Retell. |
| | If fewer than 40 words are read correctly on any passage, use professional judgment whether to administer Retell for that passage. |
| *Reminders* | If the student stops (and it's not a hesitation on a specific item), say *Keep going.* (Repeat as often as needed.) |
| | If the student loses her/his place, point. (Repeat as often as needed.) |
| *Turn page* | If student reaches the end of the page (designated by triangles in the scoring booklet) before the minute is up, turn the page and continue on the next page. Otherwise, proceed to Retell when the minute is up. |

## Planting a Butterfly Garden

some gardening dirt while you do this. Now it is time to plant. Butterfly gardens need host plants for butterflies to lay eggs on and for caterpillars to eat. They also need plants that provide nectar to feed the butterflies.

With a little time and care, you can enjoy both colorful flowers and butterflies!

# 12 DIBELS® Oral Reading Fluency
Level 3/Progress Monitoring 12 Retell

▶ *Now tell me as much as you can about the story you just read. Ready, begin.*

| | |
|---|---|
| *Timing* | 1-minute maximum. Start your stopwatch after telling the student to begin. Say **Stop** after 1 minute. |
| *Wait/ Reminder* | If the student stops or hesitates for 3 seconds, select *one* of the following (allowed one time):<br>—If the student has not said anything at all, provides a very limited response, or provides an off-track response, say **Tell me as much as you can about the story**.<br>—Otherwise, ask **Can you tell me anything more about the story?** |
| *Discontinue* | After the first reminder, if the student does not say anything or gets off track for 5 seconds, say **Thank you** and discontinue the task. |

**DORF/Level 3**

# Lan's First Day

▶ It was Lan's first day in her new school in the United States. She had left China just one week earlier, so the English words her classmates spoke sounded strange to her.

The teacher explained something and then passed out papers. Lan didn't understand what was on the papers and felt confused. She could tell that her classmates were excited about what they were reading. From their expressions, she guessed it was a story.

Some of Lan's classmates gathered at the front of the room. They talked in funny voices and made interesting expressions with their faces. Slowly, Lan realized that the students were acting out a play. Lan watched closely as a girl in a red cape skipped along and then stopped to have a conversation with a tall boy. The boy smiled in a sneaky way and growled like a wolf. "That villain is up to no good," thought Lan.

In the end, the tall boy pretended to be an old woman in bed. When the girl in the cape approached him, the boy sprang out of bed and chased her. The girl outsmarted the wolf and escaped. Right then, Lan recognized the story. It was similar to a tale her mother told her about a wolf who tricked children by pretending to be a grandmother. Lan raised

# 13 DIBELS® Oral Reading Fluency
Level 3/Progress Monitoring 13

Read the directions on page 273.

▶ **Begin testing. *Put your finger under the first word*** (point to the first word of the passage)**. *Ready, begin.***

| | |
|---|---|
| *Timing* | 1 minute. Start your stopwatch after the student says the first word of the passage. Place a bracket ( ] ) and say ***Stop*** after 1 minute. |
| *Wait* | If no response in 3 seconds, say the word and mark it as incorrect. |
| *Discontinue* | If no words are read correctly in the first line, say ***Stop***, record a score of 0, and do not administer Retell. |
| | If fewer than 40 words are read correctly on any passage, use professional judgment whether to administer Retell for that passage. |
| *Reminders* | If the student stops (and it's not a hesitation on a specific item), say ***Keep going.*** (Repeat as often as needed.) |
| | If the student loses her/his place, point. (Repeat as often as needed.) |
| *Turn page* | If student reaches the end of the page (designated by triangles in the scoring booklet) before the minute is up, turn the page and continue on the next page. Otherwise, proceed to Retell when the minute is up. |

DORF/Level 3

## Lan's First Day

her hand. "Lon Po Po!" she said excitedly.

Everyone looked at Lan in surprise. "That's right, Lan," said the teacher. "This tale is similar to the Chinese story of Lon Po Po. It's called Little Red Riding Hood."

Lan repeated the words slowly, "Little Red Riding Hood." Everyone smiled when they heard how well she spoke. Lan smiled shyly back and thought, "This school is going to be fun!"

# 13 DIBELS® Oral Reading Fluency
Level 3/Progress Monitoring 13 Retell

▶ *Now tell me as much as you can about the story you just read. Ready, begin.*

| | |
|---|---|
| **Timing** | 1-minute maximum. Start your stopwatch after telling the student to begin. Say **Stop** after 1 minute. |
| **Wait/ Reminder** | If the student stops or hesitates for 3 seconds, select *one* of the following (allowed one time): <br>—If the student has not said anything at all, provides a very limited response, or provides an off-track response, say **Tell me as much as you can about the story**. <br>—Otherwise, ask **Can you tell me anything more about the story?** |
| **Discontinue** | After the first reminder, if the student does not say anything or gets off track for 5 seconds, say **Thank you** and discontinue the task. |

# Kayla's Special Owl

▶ The wildlife center was only a few blocks away. Kayla and her family walked there almost every day. She had been visiting the center since she was two years old. Kayla loved looking at the animals and hiking the surrounding trails. What Kayla liked the very best of all, though, were the birds. This summer, she was finally old enough to volunteer in the center's bird rescue area. She couldn't wait to start.

Every week people brought wounded or abandoned birds to the center. They were cared for and then released back into the wild. After training, Kayla was ready for work. She helped clean cages and mixed up special food. Soon, she was able to work with the "babies." She fed these tiny birds by hand using a small paintbrush. She would dip the brush into water or the food mix and then gently put her hand over the bird and drop a small amount into its gaping mouth. Baby birds need to be fed every twenty minutes, so this was something the volunteers took turns doing all day long.

Of all the birds Kayla helped, her favorite was a small screech owl. She had been the first one to feed the tiny creature, and the two had formed a special bond. It needed constant attention. Kayla watched the

# 14 DIBELS® Oral Reading Fluency
Level 3/Progress Monitoring 14

Read the directions on page 273.

▶ **Begin testing.** *Put your finger under the first word* (point to the first word of the passage). *Ready, begin.*

| | |
|---|---|
| *Timing* | 1 minute. Start your stopwatch after the student says the first word of the passage. Place a bracket ( **]** ) and say *Stop* after 1 minute. |
| *Wait* | If no response in 3 seconds, say the word and mark it as incorrect. |
| *Discontinue* | If no words are read correctly in the first line, say *Stop*, record a score of 0, and do not administer Retell. |
| | If fewer than 40 words are read correctly on any passage, use professional judgment whether to administer Retell for that passage. |
| *Reminders* | If the student stops (and it's not a hesitation on a specific item), say *Keep going.* (Repeat as often as needed.) |
| | If the student loses her/his place, point. (Repeat as often as needed.) |
| *Turn page* | If student reaches the end of the page (designated by triangles in the scoring booklet) before the minute is up, turn the page and continue on the next page. Otherwise, proceed to Retell when the minute is up. |

## Kayla's Special Owl

owl get stronger every day as she cared for it. Soon, it could eat on its own and was moved from the inside care room to an outside cage for birds that would soon be released. The time came to let the little owl go. Kayla wasn't sad, though, because she somehow knew she would see her owl again. That night, she heard a hooting sound in the tree just outside her window. Her special owl was safe and near.

# 14 DIBELS® Oral Reading Fluency
Level 3/Progress Monitoring 14 Retell

▶ *Now tell me as much as you can about the story you just read. Ready, begin.*

| | |
|---|---|
| *Timing* | 1-minute maximum. Start your stopwatch after telling the student to begin. Say **Stop** after 1 minute. |
| *Wait/ Reminder* | If the student stops or hesitates for 3 seconds, select *one* of the following (allowed one time):<br>—If the student has not said anything at all, provides a very limited response, or provides an off-track response, say **Tell me as much as you can about the story**.<br>—Otherwise, ask **Can you tell me anything more about the story?** |
| *Discontinue* | After the first reminder, if the student does not say anything or gets off track for 5 seconds, say **Thank you** and discontinue the task. |

# Amazing Dolphins

▶ Can you jump as high as a house? Could you win a race with a shark? Could you find a quarter on the playground with your eyes closed? You could do all these things if you were a dolphin!

A dolphin has a very strong tail that helps it jump high in the air. A dolphin's tail muscles are much stronger than the muscles of other mammals. A dolphin pumps its tail up and down to propel itself through the water. A dolphin can swim so fast that one flick of its tail sends the dolphin sailing into the air. Jumping out of the water is one way the dolphin gets air while swimming.

Dolphins do not always swim at top speed, but they are always ready to go fast if an enemy comes near. Dolphins often swim together in a group. They warn each other if they see a shark. When escaping a shark, dolphins can swim as fast as some speedboats!

One of the most interesting things about a dolphin's body is the way it finds things. A dolphin makes clicking sounds that bounce off objects in the sea. When the clicking sounds bounce, they make echoes that the dolphin can hear. The sound of the echoes tells the dolphin where things are. Using clicks and echoes, a dolphin could find a quarter that was a

# 15 DIBELS® Oral Reading Fluency
Level 3/Progress Monitoring 15

Read the directions on page 273.

▶ **Begin testing.** *Put your finger under the first word* (point to the first word of the passage). *Ready, begin.*

| | |
|---|---|
| *Timing* | 1 minute. Start your stopwatch after the student says the first word of the passage. Place a bracket ( **]** ) and say *Stop* after 1 minute. |
| *Wait* | If no response in 3 seconds, say the word and mark it as incorrect. |
| *Discontinue* | If no words are read correctly in the first line, say *Stop*, record a score of 0, and do not administer Retell.<br><br>If fewer than 40 words are read correctly on any passage, use professional judgment whether to administer Retell for that passage. |
| *Reminders* | If the student stops (and it's not a hesitation on a specific item), say *Keep going.* (Repeat as often as needed.)<br>If the student loses her/his place, point. (Repeat as often as needed.) |
| *Turn page* | If student reaches the end of the page (designated by triangles in the scoring booklet) before the minute is up, turn the page and continue on the next page. Otherwise, proceed to Retell when the minute is up. |

## Amazing Dolphins

half a block away! The clicks and echoes are important because they help the dolphin find food. The sounds also help dolphins stay away from enemies.

When you see a dolphin jumping, swimming, and making noises you'll know it is not just playing. It is also using its amazing body to stay safe and healthy!

_____

# 15 DIBELS® Oral Reading Fluency
Level 3/Progress Monitoring 15 Retell

▶ *Now tell me as much as you can about the story you just read. Ready, begin.*

| | |
|---|---|
| **Timing** | 1-minute maximum. Start your stopwatch after telling the student to begin. Say **Stop** after 1 minute. |
| **Wait/ Reminder** | If the student stops or hesitates for 3 seconds, select *one* of the following (allowed one time):<br>—If the student has not said anything at all, provides a very limited response, or provides an off-track response, say **Tell me as much as you can about the story**.<br>—Otherwise, ask **Can you tell me anything more about the story?** |
| **Discontinue** | After the first reminder, if the student does not say anything or gets off track for 5 seconds, say **Thank you** and discontinue the task. |

DORF/Level 3

## Strawberry Festival Day

▶ At the strawberry festival, Tessa stood between her stepmom and her dad. The parade was starting. Looking down the street, Tessa was startled by one of the floats. "That's the biggest cake I've ever seen!" she exclaimed.

"I know," her stepmom answered. "I've been coming to this strawberry festival since I was your age. Every year, people use the berries they grow here. They work together to make a huge strawberry shortcake. It's always the first thing in the parade. The best part comes after the parade. That's when everyone at the festival gets to eat it!"

When the parade was over, Tessa and her parents made their way to the line for a piece of the giant strawberry shortcake. Tessa's mouth watered as she wondered what the cake would taste like. Tessa's stepmom stood in line and got them each a helping of the cake. "This is delicious," Tessa said as she ate it.

After they finished the cake, they walked around for a long time. They stopped and listened to a band in the park, and then rode a few rides. As the sun began to set, Tessa got her face painted. She smiled as she looked in the mirror at the bright red strawberry on her cheek.

# 16 DIBELS® Oral Reading Fluency
Level 3/Progress Monitoring 16

Read the directions on page 273.

▶ **Begin testing.** *Put your finger under the first word* (point to the first word of the passage). *Ready, begin.*

| | |
|---|---|
| **Timing** | 1 minute. Start your stopwatch after the student says the first word of the passage. Place a bracket ( **]** ) and say *Stop* after 1 minute. |
| **Wait** | If no response in 3 seconds, say the word and mark it as incorrect. |
| **Discontinue** | If no words are read correctly in the first line, say *Stop*, record a score of 0, and do not administer Retell.<br><br>If fewer than 40 words are read correctly on any passage, use professional judgment whether to administer Retell for that passage. |
| **Reminders** | If the student stops (and it's not a hesitation on a specific item), say *Keep going.* (Repeat as often as needed.)<br>If the student loses her/his place, point. (Repeat as often as needed.) |
| **Turn page** | If student reaches the end of the page (designated by triangles in the scoring booklet) before the minute is up, turn the page and continue on the next page. Otherwise, proceed to Retell when the minute is up. |

## Strawberry Festival Day

Tessa took her dad's hand, and with her other hand, she reached for her stepmom. They both held Tessa's hands tightly and smiled at her. They looked up at the fireworks that lit the dark sky. It was a beautiful ending to a great day.

---

# 16 DIBELS® Oral Reading Fluency
Level 3/Progress Monitoring 16 Retell

▶ *Now tell me as much as you can about the story you just read. Ready, begin.*

| | |
|---|---|
| *Timing* | 1-minute maximum. Start your stopwatch after telling the student to begin. Say **Stop** after 1 minute. |
| *Wait/Reminder* | If the student stops or hesitates for 3 seconds, select *one* of the following (allowed one time):<br>—If the student has not said anything at all, provides a very limited response, or provides an off-track response, say **Tell me as much as you can about the story**.<br>—Otherwise, ask **Can you tell me anything more about the story?** |
| *Discontinue* | After the first reminder, if the student does not say anything or gets off track for 5 seconds, say **Thank you** and discontinue the task. |

# A Poetry Contest

▶ The class listened politely as the visiting author read some of her poems. After the poet left, their teacher, Mrs. North, told them to get out their writing notebooks. Mrs. North wanted each of them to try writing a poem. Everyone started scribbling away. Everyone, that is, but Brenden. He just stared at the blank page before him, wondering what to write. Then, the bell rang. Mrs. North told them to finish their poems for homework.

As Brenden walked home from school, an idea hit him. He would write a poem about baseball! He loved baseball. At home, he sat down at his desk and started writing. Brenden's pen could barely keep up with the words tumbling out of his head. He was even able to make his words rhyme, which the guest poet had said could be difficult. The next day, Brenden turned in his poem. He hoped his teacher would like it.

A few weeks later, Mrs. North called Brenden to her desk. She told him that a local bookstore had asked teachers to enter poems, written by their students, in the store's yearly poetry contest. Brenden's poem had been selected. Mrs. North told him what a great honor this was. His poem would be published in a book along with the other selected

# 17 DIBELS® Oral Reading Fluency
Level 3/Progress Monitoring 17

Read the directions on page 273.

▶ **Begin testing.** *Put your finger under the first word* (point to the first word of the passage). *Ready, begin.*

| | |
|---|---|
| *Timing* | 1 minute. Start your stopwatch after the student says the first word of the passage. Place a bracket ( **]** ) and say *Stop* after 1 minute. |
| *Wait* | If no response in 3 seconds, say the word and mark it as incorrect. |
| *Discontinue* | If no words are read correctly in the first line, say *Stop*, record a score of 0, and do not administer Retell. |
| | If fewer than 40 words are read correctly on any passage, use professional judgment whether to administer Retell for that passage. |
| *Reminders* | If the student stops (and it's not a hesitation on a specific item), say *Keep going.* (Repeat as often as needed.) |
| | If the student loses her/his place, point. (Repeat as often as needed.) |
| *Turn page* | If student reaches the end of the page (designated by triangles in the scoring booklet) before the minute is up, turn the page and continue on the next page. Otherwise, proceed to Retell when the minute is up. |

DORF/Level 3

## A Poetry Contest

entries. Also, each poet was to read his or her poem that Saturday at the bookstore.

When Saturday came, Brenden went with his family to the bookstore. Finally, it was his turn to read. Everyone clapped after he read. When all the poems were recited, the store's manager gave out prizes. Brenden had won a gift card for having the best poem in his age group. He thought that now he might like poetry as much as he liked baseball!

---

# 17 DIBELS® Oral Reading Fluency
Level 3/Progress Monitoring 17 Retell

▶ *Now tell me as much as you can about the story you just read. Ready, begin.*

| | |
|---|---|
| **Timing** | 1-minute maximum. Start your stopwatch after telling the student to begin. Say **Stop** after 1 minute. |
| **Wait/ Reminder** | If the student stops or hesitates for 3 seconds, select *one* of the following (allowed one time):<br>　—If the student has not said anything at all, provides a very limited response, or provides an off-track response, say **Tell me as much as you can about the story**.<br>　—Otherwise, ask **Can you tell me anything more about the story?** |
| **Discontinue** | After the first reminder, if the student does not say anything or gets off track for 5 seconds, say **Thank you** and discontinue the task. |

# Keeping the Planet Clean

▶ No matter where you are in the world, you can always do your best to keep the planet clean. Throwing away trash properly is one way to do this. Recycling is another way.

People can litter without even knowing they are doing it. Sometimes, drivers put trash in roadside bins that are overly full. Before the bin gets emptied, the trash can spill out. It is then carried all over by the wind to another place. Who knows where it might end up? Almost twenty percent of our litter ends up in rivers and oceans. This affects our drinking water as well as fish and other wildlife. If you are someplace and you are not sure that the trash will be picked up, wait to throw it away in a place where you know it will not become litter.

Even when it is thrown away properly, trash is bad for the Earth. Another way to deal with trash is to make less of it. This is where recycling can help. You can ask family and friends to buy things with packaging that can be recycled or reused. You can also try to avoid paper plates and cups and instead use washable dishes that you can use again. Using reusable grocery sacks cuts down on the number of plastic bags we use and throw away.

# 18 DIBELS® Oral Reading Fluency
Level 3/Progress Monitoring 18

Read the directions on page 273.

▶ **Begin testing.** *Put your finger under the first word* (point to the first word of the passage). *Ready, begin.*

| | |
|---|---|
| *Timing* | 1 minute. Start your stopwatch after the student says the first word of the passage. Place a bracket ( **]** ) and say *Stop* after 1 minute. |
| *Wait* | If no response in 3 seconds, say the word and mark it as incorrect. |
| *Discontinue* | If no words are read correctly in the first line, say *Stop*, record a score of 0, and do not administer Retell.<br><br>If fewer than 40 words are read correctly on any passage, use professional judgment whether to administer Retell for that passage. |
| *Reminders* | If the student stops (and it's not a hesitation on a specific item), say *Keep going.* (Repeat as often as needed.)<br>If the student loses her/his place, point. (Repeat as often as needed.) |
| *Turn page* | If student reaches the end of the page (designated by triangles in the scoring booklet) before the minute is up, turn the page and continue on the next page. Otherwise, proceed to Retell when the minute is up. |

## Keeping the Planet Clean

Sometimes you will need to use things you can't recycle or reuse. The most important thing is to try to use less of this type of item. Doing your part to help keep our planet clean helps us all.

———————————————————————————

# 18 DIBELS® Oral Reading Fluency
Level 3/Progress Monitoring 18 Retell

▶ *Now tell me as much as you can about the story you just read. Ready, begin.*

| | |
|---|---|
| **Timing** | 1-minute maximum. Start your stopwatch after telling the student to begin. Say **Stop** after 1 minute. |
| **Wait/ Reminder** | If the student stops or hesitates for 3 seconds, select *one* of the following (allowed one time):<br>—If the student has not said anything at all, provides a very limited response, or provides an off-track response, say **Tell me as much as you can about the story**.<br>—Otherwise, ask **Can you tell me anything more about the story?** |
| **Discontinue** | After the first reminder, if the student does not say anything or gets off track for 5 seconds, say **Thank you** and discontinue the task. |

# How Worms Help Gardens

▶ If you want to have a beautiful garden, you should start with good dirt. Garden soil needs to be cared for just like your plants do. Worms can help you do this! Worms have been tending the soil since before the last Ice Age and can live in most places that are not too hot or cold. Most worms are only several inches long, but there are some types that can grow to be longer than a car.

There are many different worms that can help your garden. The most common is the earthworm. Earthworms eat their way through the soil, making meals out of decaying plant matter and bacteria. Their waste, called castings, helps enrich the soil. As they move through the ground, they create burrows or tunnels. This helps get more air and water into the dirt and keeps it from compacting. Plant roots can grow more easily, and water is able to stay in the soil for longer periods of time.

Another worm that can help your garden is the red wiggler. These worms don't burrow into the soil. They feed on the surface, which makes them perfect for composting. Compost is a mixture of decaying organic matter that is used to fertilize the land. It is made up of things like leaves or grass clippings. It can also include things like carrot peels and other

# 19 DIBELS® Oral Reading Fluency
Level 3/Progress Monitoring 19

Read the directions on page 273.

▶ **Begin testing.** *Put your finger under the first word* (point to the first word of the passage). *Ready, begin.*

| | |
|---|---|
| *Timing* | 1 minute. Start your stopwatch after the student says the first word of the passage. Place a bracket ( **]** ) and say *Stop* after 1 minute. |
| *Wait* | If no response in 3 seconds, say the word and mark it as incorrect. |
| *Discontinue* | If no words are read correctly in the first line, say *Stop*, record a score of 0, and do not administer Retell.<br><br>If fewer than 40 words are read correctly on any passage, use professional judgment whether to administer Retell for that passage. |
| *Reminders* | If the student stops (and it's not a hesitation on a specific item), say *Keep going.* (Repeat as often as needed.)<br><br>If the student loses her/his place, point. (Repeat as often as needed.) |
| *Turn page* | If student reaches the end of the page (designated by triangles in the scoring booklet) before the minute is up, turn the page and continue on the next page. Otherwise, proceed to Retell when the minute is up. |

DORF/Level 3

## How Worms Help Gardens

kitchen scraps. The wigglers are added to the mix, and they eat and digest the food, leaving behind their castings. Castings are then mixed into soil before it is used for planting. These worms can devour a lot of waste. One pound of wigglers can eat eight ounces of food in a day!

All in all, worms are really amazing and are truly a gardener's friend.

# 19 DIBELS® Oral Reading Fluency
Level 3/Progress Monitoring 19 Retell

▶ *Now tell me as much as you can about the story you just read. Ready, begin.*

| | |
|---|---|
| *Timing* | 1-minute maximum. Start your stopwatch after telling the student to begin. Say **Stop** after 1 minute. |
| *Wait/ Reminder* | If the student stops or hesitates for 3 seconds, select *one* of the following (allowed one time):<br>—If the student has not said anything at all, provides a very limited response, or provides an off-track response, say **Tell me as much as you can about the story**.<br>—Otherwise, ask **Can you tell me anything more about the story?** |
| *Discontinue* | After the first reminder, if the student does not say anything or gets off track for 5 seconds, say **Thank you** and discontinue the task. |

# A Chess Tournament

▶ The principal walked into the school library. She had just received a letter inviting several members of the school's chess team to play in the state championship. Rachel could hardly believe her ears when she heard her name read as one of the people who had been chosen.

The chess club met twice a week after school in the library. Rachel's teacher had suggested that she try it last year, because she knew that Rachel loved problem solving. What started out as just an interesting school activity was now something that she loved doing. Rachel had become one of the club's best players. Still, she wondered if she was good enough for this tournament.

Rachel talked it over with her parents and her teacher. They all told her that she was chosen because she was a very good player. They reminded her that no matter what the outcome was, she would enjoy the challenge of each match and would learn from every game she played. When Rachel thought about it, she realized they were right. The tournament games would just be new puzzles to solve. Rachel felt more confident.

When the tournament day arrived, Rachel was ready. After a good

# 20 DIBELS® Oral Reading Fluency
Level 3/Progress Monitoring 20

Read the directions on page 273.

▶ **Begin testing.** *Put your finger under the first word* (point to the first word of the passage). *Ready, begin.*

| | |
|---|---|
| *Timing* | 1 minute. Start your stopwatch after the student says the first word of the passage. Place a bracket ( **]** ) and say *Stop* after 1 minute. |
| *Wait* | If no response in 3 seconds, say the word and mark it as incorrect. |
| *Discontinue* | If no words are read correctly in the first line, say *Stop*, record a score of 0, and do not administer Retell. |
| | If fewer than 40 words are read correctly on any passage, use professional judgment whether to administer Retell for that passage. |
| *Reminders* | If the student stops (and it's not a hesitation on a specific item), say *Keep going.* (Repeat as often as needed.) |
| | If the student loses her/his place, point. (Repeat as often as needed.) |
| *Turn page* | If student reaches the end of the page (designated by triangles in the scoring booklet) before the minute is up, turn the page and continue on the next page. Otherwise, proceed to Retell when the minute is up. |

## A Chess Tournament

night's rest and a healthy breakfast, she arrived early to check in. Then, she played some practice games with her friends. Soon, it was time for her first match to begin. Over the next two days, she played six games. She won four, lost one, and had one tie. When the final points were tallied, she had won third place. She was thrilled, and in her heart, she knew she had won much more than a trophy.

# 20 DIBELS® Oral Reading Fluency
Level 3/Progress Monitoring 20 Retell

---

▶ *Now tell me as much as you can about the story you just read. Ready, begin.*

---

| | |
|---|---|
| *Timing* | 1-minute maximum. Start your stopwatch after telling the student to begin. Say **Stop** after 1 minute. |
| *Wait/ Reminder* | If the student stops or hesitates for 3 seconds, select *one* of the following (allowed one time):<br>—If the student has not said anything at all, provides a very limited response, or provides an off-track response, say **Tell me as much as you can about the story**.<br>—Otherwise, ask **Can you tell me anything more about the story?** |
| *Discontinue* | After the first reminder, if the student does not say anything or gets off track for 5 seconds, say **Thank you** and discontinue the task. |